I0054540

THE FAILURE PORTFOLIO

How to Turn Your Biggest Mistakes Into Your Greatest Success

Katyya Moses

THE FAILURE PORTFOLIO:

How to Turn Your Biggest Mistakes into Your Greatest Success

Copyright © 2025 by Katyya Moses

All rights reserved. No part of this publication may be reproduced, distributed, or transmitted in any form or by any means, including photocopying, recording, or other electronic or mechanical methods, without the prior written permission of the publisher, except in the case of brief quotations embodied in critical reviews and certain other noncommercial uses permitted by copyright law.

Disclaimer: The strategies shared in this book are based on personal experience and proven frameworks, but results are not guaranteed. Success depends on individual effort, action, and follow-through.

First Edition
ISBN: 979-8-9932734-1-9
Published by Katyya Moses

Contact:
[hello@elevatehervault.com/www.thefailureportfolio.com]

Printed in the United States of America

Dedication

To the moms, women, and parents who refuse to choose between building their dreams and being present for their families. May your failures become the foundation for the life you are creating.

Contents

You Were Taught to Fear the One Thing That Sets You Free

There is a lie so many of us were raised to believe: If you play it safe, work hard, and follow the rules, you'll eventually be rewarded.

We internalize it early. Color inside the lines. Get good grades. Don't ask too many questions.

We learn to chase approval instead of possibility.

To prioritize stability over joy. To settle for "secure" instead of aiming for *significant*. And when life starts to feel small or unfulfilled, we blame ourselves.

We wonder why we are exhausted and unmotivated. Why we feel called to *more* but can't seem to reach it. Why starting something new feels terrifying—even when staying the same is quietly suffocating us.

I lived in that space for years, doing what I was taught to do. Showing up. Following the rules. Waiting for it all to finally "pay off." But even then, I knew deep down I was meant to build something of my own. I never wanted to give up. And because of that, there were moments when something inside me kept saying, *you can't keep living like this. You were made for more. It's time to do what you were placed on this earth to do.*

It wasn't some grand vision or perfect strategy. Just a quiet decision: to try one more time, even though I was scared. To do something different, even if it didn't work. To stop waiting for permission and start betting on myself.

That moment changed everything. Not because the outcome was guaranteed.

But because I finally understood this: **The road to success is paved with revisions, restarts, and risks that didn't work— until they did**.

There's a shift that happens when fear stops making your decisions. You stop waiting to feel ready. You stop trying to get it perfect. You learn to move anyway—to take the next step when the map is not clear, to show up when doubt is loud, to build something meaningful while courage is still catching up. You fail smarter. You recover faster. And somewhere in the middle of all that uncertainty, you realize you are becoming someone unshakable.

If you've ever felt stuck in a life that looks fine on paper but doesn't feel like yours...

If you've ever launched something with shaky hands and a racing heart...

If you've ever failed and wondered if that meant you should quit...

This is for you.

The Great Educational Deception

Our schools have trained us to see failure as the end of the story. But failure isn't a period at the end of your sentence; it's a comma that leads to everything that matters.

Failure is the first step towards success.

Let me be honest with you from the start. As a certified teacher with a master's degree in education and certifications in both Texas and Mississippi, I spent over a decade perpetuating one of the most damaging myths in our society. I was complicit in teaching an entire generation that failure should be feared, avoided, and hidden at all costs.

For more than ten years, I stood in front of classrooms in Mississippi, Kuwait, and Texas, unconsciously reinforcing a system that prioritizes perfection over progress. Every red mark on a paper, every failed test, every disappointed look when a student got the "wrong" answer contributed to a massive deception that conditions us to believe our mistakes define our limitations rather than our potential.

The truth is this: every breakthrough, every innovation, and every moment of genuine learning happens not in spite of failure, but because of it. Yet our educational system has inverted this fundamental law of growth, creating generations of people paralyzed by the fear of being wrong.

What if I told you that this fear—this carefully conditioned terror of failure—is the very thing preventing you from achieving the success and freedom you crave?

Disillusioned Educator

My story isn't a straight line from point A to point B. It's messier, more human, and infinitely more real than the polished success stories you see on social media.

I chose to pursue a degree in education because I was being practical—what job would allow me to be home with my kids more? I graduated from college and started my Master's while being a stay-at-home mom. The plan seemed solid, sensible, and safe.

When I finally started teaching, I really hated it. I despised the system, the way we taught kids, and how creativity was suffocated by standardized testing and rigid curricula. But eventually, I fell in line.

By "fell in line," I mean I accepted that maybe this was just how life had to be. I convinced myself my discomfort was immaturity, that every adult learns to swallow their idealism and do what's expected. The traditional path, the one I'd been taught was "safe" and "secure," felt like a slow suffocation of my dreams.

Looking back, I wish someone had told me that practicality and purpose aren't the same thing. No one ever said, *"Pay attention to what you are naturally good at. What you love. What people come to you for."*

We weren't taught to build careers around our gifts. We were taught to fit into systems. When you learn how to lean into your strengths and monetize what already lives inside you, the path might still be hard, but it finally starts to make sense.

Learning to Pivot

Before fully surrendering to that suffocation, I tried something different. As a stay-at-home mom, I launched business after business, experiment after experiment. Most failed spectacularly. The most I ever made was $1,000.

I only wanted to work from home and be there for my kids. When business after business didn't take off, when the rejections piled up and the bank account remained stubbornly low, I felt defeated. It just didn't seem like I was truly living.

That's the point where it starts to feel easier to shrink back than to keep reaching. Maybe dreams are for other people. Maybe it's wiser to follow the safe route, collect the steady paycheck, and find meaning in small moments instead of bold ones. But something in me couldn't fully let it go. I didn't know it then, but I wasn't giving up. I was learning to pivot.

The Moment Everything Changed

I had already tried a handful of business ideas, and none of them took off. Most ended in disappointment, a few in complete silence. But this time, it felt different. Not because I had more experience, but because I had a different mindset. Instead of chasing perfection or waiting for the fear to disappear, I made a quiet decision: *What if I tried again anyway?* What I didn't know that night was that I was about to learn the most valuable lesson of my life: **failure isn't the opposite of success; it's the prerequisite for it.**

Over the next two years, I would discover that every "mistake" was actually data. Every setback was feedback. Every disappointment was direction.

I would learn that the very conditioning that made me afraid to fail was the same conditioning that had been keeping me stuck. That the fear of getting it wrong was the only thing stopping me from getting it right. That the need for permission was the real prison.

Why This Book Exists

I used to think fear was just part of the process. That hesitation, second-guessing, and playing small were signs of humility or responsibility. But once I stopped letting fear lead, everything changed. I discovered something I wish someone had told me sooner: When you stop being afraid to fail, you finally unlock the courage to build the life you actually want.

And here's the thing, I know I'm not the only one. Millions of teachers, moms, and career changers have been shaped by the same systems that taught me to play it safe. Systems that reward obedience, punish risk, and call it success.

This is for anyone who's ever felt boxed in by someone else's version of "enough." For the woman who's been told her dream is too big. For the mom who's been told to be grateful for a job that drains her. For the creative who buried her gift to be "realistic."

What changed my life wasn't some overnight success or lucky break. It was this: I started anyway. I kept going. I learned to use fear as a signal, not a stop sign.

If that shift could turn a stuck, fear-paralyzed teacher into someone with multiple income streams and a renewed sense of purpose—then I know it can do the same for you.

This isn't just my story. It's your roadmap to finally building the life you've been dreaming about.

Because once you stop fearing failure, nothing—and no one—can stop you.

What You'll Discover in These Pages

Throughout this book, you'll discover:

Why We're Taught to Fear Mistakes: How our school systems, despite their best intentions, create risk-averse adults paralyzed by the possibility of making mistakes.

The Science of Failing Forward: Your brain is built to learn from failure. Once you understand how, you'll stop avoiding mistakes and start using them to move faster.

My Complete Journey: Every mistake, pivot, and breakthrough that transformed my scattered attempts into a systematic approach to building sustainable income.

Finding Your Ideal Customer: Learn how to define your niche, research real problems, and create solutions that actually help people—not just take up space in your business.

Practical Frameworks: Step-by-step tools for making mistakes without shame—and turning every flop into feedback you can use.

The 30-Day Failure Challenge: A complete action plan for implementing these concepts immediately, including a guide to help you get started.

Practical Frameworks & Tools: You'll get access to multiple strategies, including the **Learning Loop**, **Failure Portfolio**, **30-Day Failure Challenge**, and the **My Business, My Baby** framework—that will help you turn setbacks into growth, take smarter risks, and build a business that matures with you. Whether you are in the newborn phase or the bold toddler years, these tools are designed to meet you where you are and move you forward with clarity and courage.

Who This Book Is For

This book is specifically written for:

Moms and Working Parents who want to build businesses that provide financial freedom and time flexibility with their families.

Teachers and Former Teachers who understand the power of learning but have been conditioned to fear failure in their own lives.

Career Changers who are tired of playing it safe and ready to bet on themselves, even if it means making mistakes along the way.

Aspiring Entrepreneurs who have been paralyzed by perfectionism and need permission to start imperfectly.

Anyone who has ever been told that failure is the opposite of success and is ready to discover the truth: failure is the fastest path to success when you know how to use it.

A Personal Promise

I promise you this: by the time you finish this book, you won't just view failure differently. You will have a complete system for transforming it into your competitive advantage.

You will walk away equipped to finally launch that business, confident enough to make those long-postponed changes, and with a clear path to the freedom you've been craving.

Most importantly, you will model something powerful for your children: that courage isn't the absence of fear or failure; it's how you respond to both. You will have built a life where you are present for what matters most.

Your Invitation to Fail Forward

As we embark on this journey together, I want you to know that every word in this book has been tested in the laboratory of real life. Every strategy has been proven not just in theory, but in practice. Every framework has been constructed from the ground up through actual failures, real mistakes, and genuine breakthroughs.

The old paradigm taught us to avoid failure. The new paradigm, which will transform your business and your life, teaches us to fail faster, braver, and with more intention than ever before.

Are you ready to discover what becomes possible when you stop fearing failure and start using it as your competitive advantage?

Are you prepared to turn your biggest mistakes into your greatest successes?

Let's begin.

PART I
THE FOUNDATION

CHAPTER 1

Built to Obey, Born to Build

How the Classroom Conditioned Us to Play Small and What It's Costing Us

I didn't always realize how deep the conditioning ran. I thought I was just doing my job—grading math tests, helping students meet expectations, praising them for getting it "right."

But the day I watched the light dim in a student's eyes over a red-marked paper, I felt a deep ache in my chest. That's when it hit me: I wasn't just teaching math. I was teaching fear. I was unintentionally training these bright, curious minds to believe that mistakes meant they weren't smart enough, that success meant staying inside the lines, and that there was only one right way to be right.

I was standing in front of my fourth-grade classroom in Kuwait, holding a stack of math tests. Red ink marked nearly every paper. Tommy had missed half the problems. He always rushed to finish first, even after I returned his paper for double-checking. Jenna ran out of time because she second-guessed everything. Essa had the correct answers but skipped steps when the directions clearly stated to show your work.

As I handed back those tests, I watched the light dim in their eyes. One by one. Test after test. Failure after failure. The grades they received didn't just mark their papers—they marked their sense of self-worth. What should have been a learning opportunity became a judgment of their intelligence, effort, and value as students.

And the truth is, failure looks different for everyone. Some of those students didn't "fail" in the traditional sense, but they felt like they did. Because failure isn't always about numbers on a page. It's about the meaning we assign to moments when we fall short of who we think we're supposed to be.

I was conditioning these beautiful, curious minds to believe that mistakes were something to be ashamed of. That not knowing something immediately meant they weren't smart enough. That there was only one right way to solve a problem.

And the most tragic part? I didn't even realize I was doing it.

I was teaching them to fear failure.

Case Study: When "Failures" Become Billionaires

Before we delve deeper into how this system conditions us, let me share something that should make every educator pause and reconsider what we're really measuring when we grade papers and rank students.

Richard Branson – Founder of Virgin Group and worth over $4 billion – was labeled a poor student due to his dyslexia. His teachers saw him as disruptive and unfocused. He dropped out of school at 16. Today, he employs thousands and has disrupted entire industries.

Barbara Corcoran – Real estate mogul and Shark Tank investor – received straight D's in school and was labeled "the dumb kid." She failed at 22 jobs before building a real estate empire worth hundreds of millions. Her "failure" to fit the academic mold became her superpower in the business world.

Bill Gates, Steve Jobs, Mark Zuckerberg – Gates was a Harvard dropout. Jobs was a Reed College dropout. Zuckerberg left Harvard to build Facebook. These aren't anomalies; they're examples of individuals who refused to let the educational system define their potential.

Jan Koum – Co-founder of WhatsApp (sold to Facebook for $19 billion) – was an immigrant who struggled with English and performed poorly in traditional academic settings. His "failure" to excel in the conventional classroom had nothing to do with his ability to understand what people needed and create solutions that would connect billions worldwide.

For every famous dropout who succeeded, how many brilliant minds never tried because they were convinced by their grades that they weren't smart enough? How many potential innovators abandoned their ideas because a red-marked paper told them they weren't capable?

The system that was supposed to identify and nurture talent was actually filtering out some of the most innovative thinkers of our time.

These individuals succeeded not despite their educational "failures," but because they learned to define success differently. They saw problems as opportunities, obstacles as catalysts for innovation, and rejection as redirection.

They learned to fail before anyone taught them that was even possible.

The Making of Risk-Averse Adults

Our educational system, despite its best intentions, operates on a fundamental flaw: the belief that learning can be measured by the absence of mistakes. We've created a factory model where success is defined as getting the "right" answer, following prescribed methods, and staying within the lines.

Think about your own school experience for a moment:

- How did you feel when you failed a test?
- What happened when you raised your hand with a "wrong" answer?
- How were you treated when you tried a different approach to solve a problem?
- What message did you receive about making mistakes?

For most of us, the message was clear: mistakes are bad, failure is the opposite of success, and the safest path is to follow the rules and avoid risks.

As a teacher with a master's degree in education, I can tell you that this isn't malicious. Teachers genuinely want their students to succeed. But the system we operate within—with its standardized tests, rigid curricula, and one-size-fits-all metrics—forces us to prioritize conformity over creativity, memorization over innovation, and safety over courage.

Red Ink Trauma: The Psychology of Educational Conditioning

Let me share something most people don't realize: the way we grade papers and tests creates a form of psychological conditioning that follows us for decades.

When I was grading those math tests with my red pen, I thought I was helping students learn from their mistakes. But research in educational psychology shows us something different. Every red mark on a paper triggers a small stress response. Every failed test activates the same neural pathways as social rejection. Every disappointed look from a teacher sends a message that mistakes equal inadequacy.

In fact, a study by Dr. Abraham Rutchick, a psychology professor at California State University, found that red ink not only lowered student motivation but also made teachers more likely to grade more harshly. The color alone has been shown to trigger anxiety responses that interfere with learning and confidence. In his research, even the simple act of picking up a red pen led graders to focus more on errors than strengths—proving that something as small as color choice can shape outcomes in powerful ways. We're literally training children's brains to associate learning with fear, experimentation with punishment, and failure with personal worth.

Dr. Carol Dweck's groundbreaking research on growth mindset versus fixed mindset shows us just how damaging this can be. When children are praised for being "smart" rather than for working hard, and when they're punished for wrong answers instead of celebrated for trying new approaches, we create what she calls a "fixed mindset"—the belief that you are either good at something or you are not, and that failure is a sign you are just not good enough. But here's what really gets me: as teachers, we often model this same fear of failure in our own lives. How many educators do you know who have stayed in jobs they hate because it's "safe"? How many have dreams of starting businesses or pursuing passions but are paralyzed by the fear of not succeeding immediately?

We teach what we know, and if we've been conditioned to fear failure, we pass that fear along to our students.

The Hidden Cost of Playing It Safe

By the time I stepped into my own classroom, I already knew the system was broken. I had felt it as a student, questioned it during my studies, and resented it from the sidelines. But nothing prepared me for what it would feel like to become part of it.

I started out with frustration—even fire. I wanted to teach differently. I wanted to reach kids, not just test them. But when creativity clashed with curriculum, when passion got buried under policies, I stopped fighting.

I conformed—just to survive.

Because the system had taught me that challenging the established way of doing things was risky. That speaking up about problems made you a troublemaker. That trying something different might fail, and failure was unacceptable.

So, I handed out red-marked papers. I followed the prescribed curriculum. I prepared students for standardized tests and checked every box, even as it emptied me.

All the while, I was dying a slow death inside.

Later, the irony wasn't lost on me: I was teaching children to fear failure while being afraid to fail myself. I urged them to follow their dreams while abandoning my own. I encouraged them to think outside the box while I remained trapped inside mine.

But the deepest damage wasn't just what the system did to me; it was what I did to myself afterward. For years, I accepted that maybe this was just how life had to be. I convinced myself that wanting more was selfish, that dreaming bigger was unrealistic, and that settling for security was the responsible thing to do.

I became my own prison guard, forcing the rules of a system I knew I'd never retire from. Teaching was never my passion. I didn't see myself doing it for 30 years, and I wasn't planning for that kind of finish line. What I *was* trying to figure out was this: What's next for me? What's the thing I'm meant to be doing?

I had already tried other paths—like Forex. I picked it up quickly, had real wins, and got excited. But when I hit a loss that felt too big, I quit. I didn't yet understand that my mistakes weren't the end—they were data. And as a teacher, I knew better. We track, assess, adjust. But I wasn't applying that same mindset to my own life.

Instead, I stayed stuck trading my time, my most valuable asset, for a paycheck I couldn't grow. I told myself it was "secure," but I knew it wasn't. One admin change, one policy shift, and everything could crumble.

The real cost? Not just a limited paycheck—but the years I spent playing small while others with fewer credentials built wealth and freedom. Why? Because they tried. They understood something I didn't yet: the biggest risk isn't just failure. It's staying stuck in something you know isn't meant for you.

The Classroom-to-Corporate Pipeline

Here's where it gets really insidious: the same conditioning that creates risk-averse students produces risk-averse adults. The system that punishes mistakes in school cultivates employees who fear innovation, hesitate to speak up, and avoid trying new approaches.

Think about it:

In School:

- Follow instructions exactly or get marked down.
- The teacher has all the answers; don't question authority.
- Work alone; collaborate when told.
- One right answer, one right method.
- Mistakes are failures to be avoided.

In Business:

- Innovation comes from questioning the status quo.
- Success requires challenging conventional wisdom.
- Collaboration and networking are essential for growth.

- Multiple solutions and infinite approaches lead to breakthroughs.
- Mistakes are data points that guide you toward success.

Do you see the disconnect?

The very habits that made us "good students"—obedient, quiet, precise—are often the exact ones that keep us stuck as adults. We're trained to follow rules, not question them. To strive for perfection, not progress. To wait for permission instead of trusting our own voice.

And it runs deeper than behavior; it shapes identity.

As children, we were praised for being compliant, not creative. We were rewarded for coloring inside the lines, not for imagining a new picture entirely. Over time, many of us learned to equate our worth with how well we followed the script. So, when it comes time to take a risk or start something of our own, we freeze—not because we're incapable, but because we've been conditioned to believe that staying safe equals being successful.

We carry those same "A-student" mindsets into adulthood— quietly asking for directions in a world that rewards those who make their own maps.

That's why so many brilliant, educated people feel stuck. They weren't taught to build.
They were taught to obey.

Yet we wonder why so many intelligent, educated individuals struggle to break free from traditional employment and build their own businesses.

The College Conditioning Trap

And the conditioning doesn't stop after high school. By the time we reach college, it is nearly complete.

We're taught to believe that success only happens in slow, structured steps. That no matter how hard you work, your growth must follow a preset timeline: Freshman, Sophomore, Junior, Senior.

You can pour your heart into every assignment, stay up until 3 AM studying, take on extra classes, and still—at the end of that year—you are just a sophomore. Maybe you graduate early, but only by completing more of the *same assigned work* in less time.

There's no real reward for acceleration. No room for exponential growth. No permission to leap.

And that, right there, is the lie that silently undermines entrepreneurs:

It teaches us that success must be earned slowly and incrementally and only after someone else says we have "earned" it.

But entrepreneurship doesn't play by those rules. If you show up, bet on yourself, and take bold, strategic action, you can generate in one year what some degrees promise in a decade. You can earn six figures, seven figures, or more—not because you followed a syllabus, but because you solved a real problem and moved with purpose.

College teaches you to wait. Business rewards you for deciding.

And that mindset doesn't just disappear when you graduate. You carry it into your career, your decisions, and your dreams, often without even realizing it. It's why so many brilliant, educated people stay stuck. Not because they lack ambition, but because they have been trained to believe they must wait for permission, even to pursue their own potential.

The Special Education Revelation

It wasn't until I moved into special education and intervention work that I began to see the cracks in the system and the possibilities beyond it.

Working with students who struggled in traditional classrooms forced me to get creative. These kids needed different approaches, timelines, and measures of success. They taught me that there isn't just one way to learn, think, or solve problems.

More importantly, they revealed that some of our most brilliant minds think differently, don't fit the mold, and challenge conventional methods. The students who struggled most in traditional settings often had the most innovative solutions when given the freedom to explore.

I started to realize that the system wasn't just failing students who learned differently—it was failing all of us by enforcing narrow definitions of success and intelligence.

When I became an intervention specialist in Kuwait, I loved it because I was finally outside the traditional classroom structure. I could create my own schedule, design individualized approaches, and celebrate progress rather than perfection.

For the first time in my teaching career, I felt like I was genuinely helping kids learn rather than forcing them to conform.

The Entrepreneur's Dilemma

But even as I learned to think differently in my professional life, I remained trapped by the same conditioning in my personal entrepreneurial attempts.

I didn't recognize it at the time, but I was still operating under the same rules I'd learned in school. Rules that had quietly followed me into adulthood.

If you don't succeed immediately, you must not be good enough. If you don't get the "right" answer quickly, it means you are doing it wrong. If things get uncertain, it's safer to quit and find something more predictable.

I was applying classroom logic to business building:

- **Expecting immediate results** (like getting an A on a test).
- **Looking for the "one right way"** to build a business (like following a formula to solve a math problem).
- **Avoiding Anything That Felt Uncertain** (like dodging difficult questions on an exam)
- **Giving Up When Things Didn't Work Perfectly** (like a student who stops trying after a few wrong answers)

The conditioning was so deep that I didn't even recognize it. I thought I was being practical, realistic, and responsible. I wasn't just following bad habits; I was following programming that was never designed to create entrepreneurs in the first place.

The Emotional Erosion

But the financial cost was nothing compared to what compromising my values did to my spirit.

Have you ever felt like you are living someone else's life? Like you are an actor playing a role that doesn't fit, saying lines that don't feel authentic, performing for an audience that doesn't really see you?

That was my reality for years. I sat in faculty meetings, nodding along with initiatives I knew could be harmful to students. I implemented curricula I did not believe in. I prepared kids for tests that measured nothing meaningful about their potential or worth.

Every day, I betrayed what I stood for in small ways. And each small betrayal chipped away at the real me.

The worst part? I started convincing myself that all of this was maturity. That settling was wisdom. That abandoning my dreams was just being "realistic."

I wasn't being responsible, but I was slowly fading. One compromise at a time.

The Relationship Ripple Effect

This quiet resignation doesn't just affect you; it seeps into every relationship in your life.

Through my actions, I was teaching my children that dreaming big was dangerous. That safety was more valuable than significance. That it's better to accept whatever life hands you than to fight for something more.

My husband would bring up old business ideas, and I'd brush them off: "That was just a phase." What I was really saying was, "I have let go of believing in myself right now, and I need you to let go too so I don't feel so ashamed."

I remember when my son asked how the *How to Hire Your Kid* course sales were going. I laughed and said, "If I advertised it, I could get more sales." But deep down, I knew I had already given up. He nodded and walked away, and in that moment, I realized I had just taught him that when something gets hard, you make excuses instead of finding solutions.

I was modeling learned helplessness. My children were watching me shrink, settle, and choose fear over faith daily. And they were learning that this is what adulthood looks like: giving up and calling it noble. The impact was deeper than I imagined. My silence, my smallness, my resignation—they weren't just limiting me. They were shaping what the people I loved believed was possible for them too.

The Identity Crisis

Perhaps the most insidious cost of conformity was what it did to my sense of self.

When you spend years ignoring your instincts, suppressing your creativity, and following someone else's blueprint for your life, you begin to lose touch with who you really are. Your authentic voice gets buried under layers of "should" and "supposed to."

I remember looking in the mirror one morning and not recognizing the woman staring back at me. When had I become so... beige? When had I stopped having opinions that mattered? When had I traded my fire for this dull, gray existence?

I was suffering from what is now called "conformity amnesia." I had forgotten what I was capable of, what I was passionate about, and what made me feel alive. I had become so adept at meeting others' expectations that I lost track of my own.

The person I had become was safe, acceptable, predictable, and completely artificial. She was a construct of the system, not an expression of my soul.

As I lost touch with who I was, I also lost sight of the opportunities life kept offering me.

Living Small in a World Full of Chances

While I played it safe, life continued to present opportunities I was too conditioned to see or too afraid to embrace:

- Every parent who inquired about tutoring services—a potential business I never started.
- Every conversation where I shared solutions to problems other teachers faced—consulting opportunities I never pursued.
- Every time I helped someone organize their finances during tax season. It could have been a service I could have expanded.

Opportunities were everywhere, but my conditioning had made me blind to them. I had been trained to see security in following the prescribed path, not in creating my own.

I was living in an opportunity-rich environment with an opportunity-poor mindset.

The Physical Toll

The stress of living inauthentically affects not just your emotions but also your body.

I was constantly tired, not from hard work, but from resisting my true nature. I expended enormous amounts of energy suppressing who I really was while maintaining a persona that felt foreign.

Sleep became elusive as my mind raced at night, whispering about all the things I wasn't doing, all the chances I wasn't taking, and all the life I wasn't living.

My health suffered as stress hormones flooded my system. The stress of suppressing who you really are differs from the stress of challenge. It's the stress of stagnation, of potential energy with nowhere to go.

I was experiencing what researchers call "learned helplessness depression"—not due to difficult external circumstances, but from the internal acceptance that things would never change.

The Generational Impact

The most heartbreaking cost was realizing that my choice to play it safe wasn't just limiting *my* future; it was quietly capping the potential of the next generation.

My children were watching me accept less than I deserved.

And yes, I was constantly encouraging them. *Be strong. Chase your dreams. Start your own business. Be brave.* I said all the right things, but they were also watching. Watching me wrestle with doubt. Watching me settle. Watching me shrink myself in real time.

Without meaning to, I was modeling a version of adulthood where dreams stay on the shelf, risk feels irresponsible, and survival gets mistaken for success. They were learning, not through my words but through my *life*, that adulthood means ignoring your purpose. That you don't take risks. That you don't believe in your own power to create change.

But here's the part we rarely acknowledge: When you are not living in your purpose, something inside of you begins to unravel. Not all at once. Not loudly. But slowly and silently.

There's a quiet ache that no title or achievement can silence. You feel it in the pit of your stomach. In your quietest moments. It's the tension between who you are and who you've settled to be.

That's what a fixed mindset does. It builds invisible walls around your potential. It whispers that you are not ready, that you are too much, that you'll fail if you try.

And over time, those whispers don't just shape your decisions. They shape your identity.

And it doesn't stop with you. That inner war spills into how you parent. How you lead.
How you speak or don't speak about your own dreams.

I was inadvertently teaching them that the world happens *to* you, not *through* you.

That you should be grateful for whatever crumbs you are offered instead of bold enough to bake your own bread. That shrinking was noble.

The play-it-safe mindset was spreading, and I was the primary carrier in my own household.

But once I saw it, I couldn't unsee it. And once I felt the weight of what I was passing down, I knew something had to change.

Not just for me, but for them.

The Breaking Point

But here's what I've learned about playing it safe: the cost compounds quietly, daily, until it becomes unbearable.

Every time you choose safety over significance, you are not preserving the status quo. You are drifting further from the life you are meant to live. Every time you ignore your instincts, you are abandoning your potential. Every time you silence your desires to fit someone else's mold, you are not staying grounded. You are surrendering your voice.

This kind of self-betrayal doesn't demand a lump sum. It takes micro payments every single day, with interest. Until eventually, something breaks.

And that debt? It shows up everywhere.

It shows up in your **wealth**—in the opportunities you don't seize, the income that never grows, and the financial stress you silently carry.

It shows up in your **health**—in the tension you hold in your body, the exhaustion that sleep can't cure, and the anxiety that hums under your skin.

It shows up in your **behavior**—in the words you swallow, the dreams you delay, and the way you shrink just enough to keep everyone comfortable.

This isn't a sudden collapse. It's a slow erosion.

It doesn't crash in like a storm. It seeps in like a quiet leak, weakening your foundation until what once felt solid begins to crack.

First, you lose your voice. Then, your fire. And finally, your belief that change is even possible.

I know because I lived it. I carried that silent ache, the feeling that I was made for more but molded for less. I didn't have a grand plan yet. I just knew I couldn't keep paying this price with my life.

That's when the shift began. Not because the world got easier. Not because the fear disappeared. But because I realized the true danger wasn't in failing. It was in continuing to live a life that didn't feel like mine.

And that realization? It was the turning point. The first crack of light through everything I thought I had to be.

Breaking the Conditioning

The first step in moving forward is recognizing that we have been trained to shrink, to avoid risk, to mistake comfort for safety, and to choose approval over possibility.

But conditioning can be undone. Neural pathways can be rewired. Habits can be reshaped. Boldness can be practiced.

It begins with a new perspective: Failure isn't a red flag; it's a stepping stone. Mistakes aren't proof you are unqualified; they are how you grow. Those uncertainties are an invitation to keep going.

The antidote is everything school never taught you: how to follow your instincts, take action before you feel ready, and stay in motion even when the outcome is unknown.

Choosing Your Future Over Your Past

Each day offers a decision: stay tethered to who you've been or step toward who you are becoming.

You are not bound to your old habits, your former limits, or anyone's expectations of who you "should" be. The ideas you've shelved, the ambitions you've quieted, the life you imagine when no one's watching—it's all still within reach.

You don't need to be fearless to move forward. You just need to be *willing* to take the first step, to risk being seen, and to try again when it doesn't go as planned.

Growth won't always look graceful. But it will be worth it.

And it starts right here with your next brave choice.

CHAPTER 2
Failure Is Not the F-Word, Fear Is

Fear Is the Real Four-Letter Word

If fear is the real four-letter word, then curiosity is the cure.

It's not the fall that keeps us from building the life we want; it's the fear of falling. The fear of doing it wrong. The fear of being seen. That's what stops smart, capable women—moms, teachers, career-changers—from ever starting.

When we stop treating failure like a dead end and start treating it like data, something shifts. We become less afraid. Not because fear disappears, but because we finally have a way to face it.

A way to *work with* it. This next part will show you how. How to spot fear in real time.
How to interrupt its grip. How to respond with clarity, courage, and power instead of paralysis.

So, let's stop running from failure and start calling out the real problem: **fear**.

What Failure Actually Is: Data, Not Defeat

Ahmed had been labeled as "failing math." On paper, his scores were low, and during independent work, he often rushed through problems, skipped steps, and made careless mistakes.

But in small groups, I noticed something different: he usually got the right answers. So, what was really happening?

I started paying closer attention. What I saw was that Ahmed wasn't just guessing. He had a *system*—a mental process that made sense to him, even if it didn't match the format his teacher expected. He was using strategies beyond his grade level but rushing to get to the answer, often without showing his work.

To an outsider, his papers looked incomplete or incorrect. But when I sat next to him and said, *"Let's work this one together,"* as he was completing the problem, I realized he wasn't confused at all. He had his own way of solving the problem, and it actually made sense. He just wasn't slowing down enough to catch small mistakes because he chose not to write out his steps the way the teacher expected. Here's the thing: we've all acquired skills that we *think* we're doing right or that we've grown confident in. But that doesn't mean those skills are without flaws or gaps.

Thinking back on it, that conversation changed the way I viewed not just Ahmed but failure itself. Ahmed wasn't failing math. The system was failing to recognize how his brain worked. And that distinction—that failure isn't final but informational—is everything.

Failure is feedback. It's data. It tells us where something's misaligned, not that we're incapable. It shows us what to tweak, not that we should give up.

What Ahmed needed wasn't more correction; it was translation. A new way to bridge what he *knew* with what the system expected. Once he understood the value of slowing down and making his thinking visible, his grades began to reflect what had been true all along: he was capable. He just needed space to learn in a way that honored how his mind worked.

How often do we do the same thing in life? Rush toward the "answer," mask our real process, and when we miss the mark, internalize it as personal failure? That moment in Kuwait reminded me: real failure is refusing to examine the data. Refusing to ask, *What can I learn here?*

Every mistake carries a message. Every setback holds insight. And when we listen instead of judge, that's where growth begins.

The Real Definition of Failure

In the real world, outside the artificial construction of our educational system, failure has a completely different meaning:

Failure is not a verdict; it's a diagnosis.

Failure is not an ending; it's an edit.

Failure is not a judgment; it's a GPS recalculating your route.

Think of a business that didn't take off or a product launch that went nowhere. These moments aren't dead ends; they are detours with feedback. They are the market handing you data on a silver platter, pointing out what didn't resonate so you can inch closer to what will.

Let me give you an example.

When I launched my first Etsy shop, I made just $1,200 in an entire year. A slow, frustrating year. The old version of the one trained by red pens and report cards read that number like a failing grade. I assumed I didn't have what it took to succeed in business.

But here's the truth I see now:

That $1,200 was never failure. It was education.

It taught me more than any overpriced business course ever could. I learned exactly which products people clicked on and which ones they ignored. I saw firsthand how Etsy's algorithm reacts to different keywords, titles, and tags. I figured out what kind of messaging made people stop scrolling and what made them keep going.

I learned how long things actually take when you are doing them yourself. I learned how to keep going when sales were slow, how to shift when things didn't click, and how to listen—really listen—to what the data was trying to tell me.

That $1,200 wasn't a loss. It was tuition.

It was the price of becoming who I needed to be to succeed. It wasn't wasted effort. It was the foundation. It didn't disqualify me but prepared me.

And that's what failure really is: not a stop sign, but a signal. A message. A teacher in disguise.

The Myth of Overnight Success: Deconstructing Entrepreneurial Fairy Tales

One of the most damaging myths in our culture is the story of overnight success. Social media has exacerbated this, showing us only the highlight reels of entrepreneurial journeys while obscuring the years of struggle, adjustment, and failure that preceded the breakthrough.

Let me burst a few bubbles for you:

Amazon: Jeff Bezos didn't turn a profit for seven years after founding Amazon in 1994. Analysts called it "Amazon.bomb," but those seven years of "failure" were actually the foundation phase.

Oprah Winfrey: Fired from her first television job for being "too emotionally invested," she used each rejection to learn about authentic communication. That emotional investment eventually made her the most trusted voice in media.

Pandora: Rejected by venture capitalists 300 times, founder Tim Westergren went without pay for two years before finally breaking through—proof that rejection is just part of the testing phase.

Spanx: Sara Blakely spent two years being told "no" by manufacturers and retailers with just $5,000 in savings. Those rejections taught her everything she needed to know about manufacturing, marketing, and retail relationships.

WhatsApp: Jan Koum and Brian Acton faced rejection from Facebook and Twitter for jobs, then used that experience to build WhatsApp—which sold to Facebook for $19 billion.

Madam C.J. Walker: Born into poverty and working as a washerwoman for $1.50 a day, her hair loss from stress became her market research opportunity. She became America's first female self-made millionaire by turning personal struggle into business insight.

Daymond John: Started FUBU with $40 and faced rejection from every major retailer for years, nearly going bankrupt multiple times. Each "no" taught him more about retail relationships, leading to over $6 billion in sales.

Every "overnight success" story is actually a decade in the making. The only thing that happened overnight was the world's attention. The success was built on a foundation of thousands of micro-failures, adjustments, and improvements.

Here's what really happens in successful businesses:

- **Year 1:** Figure out what doesn't work (looks like failure)
- **Year 2:** Refine based on what you learned (still looks like failure)
- **Year 3:** Find your groove but struggle with scale (getting warmer)
- **Year 4:** Systems start working but profitability is elusive (almost there)
- **Year 5:** Breakthrough moment that everyone calls "overnight success"

The myth of overnight success is particularly damaging for early entrepreneurs because it makes us feel "behind" or "not good enough" when our businesses don't explode immediately.

But here's the truth: there is no "behind." There's only learning. There's only growth. Every step, even the messy ones, is information you can use to move forward.

The key is recognizing the lesson and recognizing it quickly. When you can do that, you can make a shift. You can implement something new. And the next time a challenge shows up, you won't be starting from scratch; you'll be equipped. You will have tools in your tool belt that help you respond with clarity and confidence.

Failure vs. Quitting: Understanding the Crucial Difference

This is where most people get confused, and it's crucial to understand the difference between failing and quitting.

Failing is when you try something, it doesn't work, you learn from it, and you adjust your approach.

Quitting is when you try something, it doesn't work, and you stop trying altogether.

Think of it like climbing a mountain: failing is slipping and catching yourself; quitting is walking back to base camp.

Failing is part of the process. Quitting is abandoning the process.

Let me give you a concrete example from my journey:

When my first Etsy shop wasn't generating the income I wanted, I had two choices:

1. **Quit:** Close the shop, convince myself that "online business isn't for me," and resign myself to thinking that "maybe this is just how life has to be."
2. **Fail forward:** Analyze what wasn't working, research better approaches, and apply what I learned to a new attempt.

I chose option two. I didn't quit; I pivoted.

When I opened my second shop, I was starting from education, data, and the failure my first shop provided.

From the quiet data that only shows up when you are willing to look honestly at what didn't work. That first shop was never a waste; it was training.

It gave me the time and space to understand the market, to learn what people actually wanted, and to discover what I *actually enjoyed selling*. Without the pressure to create everything, I could focus on refining instead of rushing.

I wasn't hustling blindly anymore; I was building with intention. That's the beauty of failing forward: it doesn't set you back. It sets you up. Every successful entrepreneur has a graveyard of failed experiments behind them. The difference isn't that they don't fail; it's that they don't let failure mean the end.

Thomas Edison didn't fail 1,000 times before inventing the light bulb—he discovered 1,000 ways that didn't work, bringing him closer to the way that did.

Dyson created 5,126 prototypes before perfecting his revolutionary vacuum cleaner. He didn't see the first 5,125 as failures—he viewed them as steps in the process.

The Wright Brothers didn't achieve flight on their first attempt. Their early flying machines crashed, broke, and failed to get off the ground. But each crash taught them something about aerodynamics, engine power, and control, bringing them closer to success.

The crucial mindset shift is this: in entrepreneurship, failure is not what stands in the way of success; it clears the path to it.

My Journey: From $1,200 to $32K — How Failure Built My Breakthrough

When I started my first Etsy shop, I had big dreams, but my effort didn't match them.

My results were underwhelming, and honestly, they mirrored the scattered energy I poured in through all the confusion. Still, I got started. And that mattered. In that first year, I made just over $1,200. It was disappointing. But it wasn't the end.

Because that $1,200 wasn't just income; it was insight.

I didn't walk away. I leaned in. I studied what didn't work. I got honest with myself. And I made a decision: Next time, I would build smarter.

That decision changed everything. In February 2024, I opened a new shop with a new mindset.

By March, I had my first sale. And before the year was over, I had earned over $32,000 as a mom, with very little ads, no team, and no viral videos.

Let me show you how that happened, starting with what felt like failure.

The $1,200 "Failure" Education

Here's what that first year taught me:

Product Selection Failure: I created products I thought were clever instead of products people actually wanted. Lesson learned: customer research beats creative assumptions every time.

Pricing Failure: I underpriced because I didn't value my own work. Lesson learned: if you don't believe your products are worth good money, neither will your customers.

Consistency Failure: I added products sporadically whenever I "felt inspired." Lesson learned: algorithms reward consistency, and customers need reliability.

Marketing Failure: I hoped people would just find my products organically. Lesson learned: "if you build it, they will come" only works in movies.

SEO Failure: I used keywords I thought sounded good instead of those people actually searched for. Lesson learned: hope is not a marketing strategy.

Each of these "failures" was actually a lesson disguised as disappointment. So no, that $1,200 wasn't profit; it was **tuition**. A year-long crash course in how the online business world *really* works.

The February 2024 Decision

By **February 2024**, I knew I had two choices: keep doing what I had been doing or get serious about building a business that actually worked. I chose the second.

But this time, I wasn't guessing. I wasn't winging it. This time, I approached everything differently:

Instead of guessing what people wanted, I researched trending keywords and analyzed successful shops in my niche to see what was already selling and why.

Instead of creating everything from scratch, I pre-made templates and products that allowed me to test ideas quickly, save time, and focus on what really moved the needle.

Instead of posting sporadically, I committed to consistent daily action, even if some days that only meant 30 minutes. I stopped waiting for inspiration and started building momentum.

Instead of hoping for organic discovery, I learned how to market my products using Pinterest, Etsy SEO, and social media. I stopped hiding and started showing up.

Instead of underpricing, I studied what top sellers were charging and positioned my products to reflect their true value because confidence in your pricing starts with confidence in your product.

And because I made those shifts, everything changed.

The March Breakthrough

My first sale in March 2024 wasn't the start of my success; it was the **culmination** of fifteen months of educational "failures." That one sale represented:

- Twelve months of market research from my initial shop
- Two months of refined strategy implementation
- Countless hours studying successful competitors
- Multiple iterations of product descriptions, pricing, and positioning
- A completely rebuilt understanding of online customer psychology

The sale itself was small; I think it was $9. But it meant everything. It proved that all my "failures" had been leading to something real.

But let's be clear: I was still figuring it out. Yes, I had my first breakthrough, but I was still navigating a new market and learning how to operate in unfamiliar territory.

I was using pre-made templates and products, but I had to learn how to use them properly, understanding licensing terms, editing requirements, and the expectations that came with selling digital products I didn't create from scratch. There were still tweaks to make, lessons to absorb, and systems to improve.

In other words, it was imperfectly perfect. The progress was real, but so was the learning curve.

Breakthroughs don't mean the work is done; they just mean you are on the right path.

The Multiplication Effect

What happened next was what entrepreneurs often call the "hockey stick" effect. It is slow, steady growth followed by rapid acceleration. But this wasn't luck or magic. It was the compound effect of all my previous failures finally paying dividends.

- By **April**, I reached **$500 in sales** because I had started to understand which products truly resonated with my audience.
- By **May**, I hit **$1,200** because I had learned how to optimize for Etsy's algorithm and positioned my listings more strategically.

- **June** brought in **$2,800**, not because of some viral moment but because my Etsy SEO strategy was working and repeat customers started coming back.
- In **July**, I crossed **$4,000** as my pricing strategy finally aligned with the value I was offering and I stopped undercharging out of fear.

With each passing month, I wasn't just earning more. I was witnessing the cumulative effect of every lesson, every mistake, and every decision finally take root.

By the end of 2024, I had generated over $32,000 in revenue. But here's the part I want you to remember: That success wasn't built on avoiding failure. It was built on refusing to quit when things didn't work the first time.

Every month brought new challenges, unexpected turns, and plenty of things that still didn't go according to plan. The difference? I no longer saw them as reasons to stop; I saw them as data points, not dead ends.

Because once you stop seeing failure as personal, you start seeing it as powerful.

The Overwhelm "Failures"

Even success brought its own set of instructive failures:

System Overload Failure: As sales increased, my manual processes couldn't keep up. I was overwhelmed with order fulfillment and customer service. Lesson learned: success without systems is unsustainable.

Multi-Shop Mistake: Thinking more shops meant more money, I opened multiple Etsy shops simultaneously. This split my focus and diluted my brand strength. Lesson learned: depth beats breadth in the early stages.

Perfectionism Paralysis: Some days, I was so overwhelmed by growth that I couldn't post anything new. Lesson learned: done is better than perfect, especially when building momentum.

Burnout Warning: I was working at every available moment, sacrificing family time for business growth. Lesson learned: sustainable success requires sustainable practices. Eventually, I established "office hours" for myself, no longer working past 7 p.m. to protect the life I was building this business for in the first place. While I didn't always adhere to it when deadlines loomed, it helped me realize the need for balance.

Each of these "failures" taught me crucial lessons about scaling, systems, focus, and work-life integration that I wouldn't have learned if everything had gone perfectly.

Cultural Differences: How Other Cultures View Failure and Risk

One of the most eye-opening aspects of my teaching experience in Kuwait was observing how different cultures approach failure and risk-taking. This perspective shift was crucial in helping me redefine my own relationship with failure.

American Failure Phobia

In American culture, we live in a strange paradox. We celebrate entrepreneurial success stories: headline-making wins, viral launches, and million-dollar milestones, while quietly shaming the failures that make those stories possible.

We crave the outcome but resist the process.

Our educational system teaches us to avoid mistakes at all costs. Get the right answer. Stay inside the lines. Don't mess up. Much like in school, our corporate culture often praises those who follow the rules under "risk management," not those who take bold steps and evolve through trial and error.

But that process? That's where we *become*. We don't get the outcome *instead of* the progress. We get the outcome *because of* the progress. That kind of progress isn't glamorous. It's messy. It's imperfect. It often *looks* like failure: missed goals, flopped launches, and wrong turns.

But it's shaping us into the kind of person who can carry the weight of the success we're asking for. You can't shortcut the growth. You can't download the becoming. You have to *live* it.

We can't just want the results; we have to become the kind of person who can *earn*, *hold*, and *keep* them. And that becoming only happens through risk, trial, missteps, and persistence.

Success isn't the absence of failure. It's the result of refusing to stop when failure shows up and learning from it instead.

Middle Eastern Perspectives

During my time in Kuwait, I noticed a different approach to business failure among local entrepreneurs. Many came from trading families where business ups and downs were viewed as natural cycles, not personal indictments.

Fatimah, a local business owner I knew, had started and closed three different ventures before finding success with her fourth. When I asked her about it, she shrugged and said, "In the first three businesses, I just did what I thought was popular, what I assumed the market needed. I had initial success, but eventually, my sales started declining. The fourth time around, I made sure to really look at what people actually needed." This approach helped her build a much more successful business. This was wisdom. She understood the cost of learning how to succeed.

Asian Resilience Models

Japan: There's a concept called "nana korobi ya oki"—fall seven times, rise eight. This philosophy is embedded in their business culture. Japanese entrepreneurs expect failure as part of the journey, not as evidence that the journey should end.

China: Failure is often viewed as "paying your dues" before earning the right to succeed. Jack Ma, founder of Alibaba, was rejected from dozens of jobs, including KFC (he was the only one out of 24 applicants not hired). He was turned down by Harvard ten times. Chinese business culture sees these rejections not as personal failures but as market education.

European Pragmatism

Germany: There's a concept called "Fehlerkultur," which literally means "error culture." It refers to the systematic approach of learning from mistakes. German businesses often encourage employees to document and share their failures so the entire organization can learn from them.

Scandinavian Countries: Failure is normalized to the extent that "failure parties" are common in startup communities. Entrepreneurs celebrate what they learned from failed ventures before moving on to new projects. In **Finland**, there's even a national **"Failure Day"** where founders share their flops publicly, while in **Norway**, events like **"Fuckup Nights"** invite entrepreneurs to laugh, reflect, and learn from their biggest mistakes.

Indigenous Wisdom

Many indigenous cultures have philosophies that directly contradict our Western failure phobia:

Native American Traditions: Often include the belief that you must fail at something seven times before you can truly master it. Each failure is seen as a necessary step in the learning process, not as evidence of inadequacy.

Australian Aboriginal Cultures: Have "walkabout" traditions where young people are expected to get lost, make mistakes, and find their own way, both literally and figuratively. The failures encountered during walkabout are considered essential for developing wisdom and self-reliance.

What We Can Learn

These cultural perspectives reveal a crucial insight: American fear of failure isn't universal or necessary. It's a learned behavior that can be unlearned.

Cultures that normalize failure tend to foster more innovative entrepreneurs, resilient businesses, and adaptive economies. When failure is destigmatized, people are more willing to experiment, more likely to innovate, and better equipped to bounce back from setbacks.

The lesson for American entrepreneurs, especially those conditioned by risk-averse educational and corporate systems, is this: failure is not a character flaw; it's a cultural construct. And constructs can be reconstructed.

Rebuilding Your Failure Framework

If you fear failure, you are not broken; you are simply using outdated software. The good news is that mental software can be updated.

Start by borrowing wisdom from cultures with healthier relationships to failure:

Adopt the Japanese approach: Expect to fall seven times. Plan for it. Budget for it. Accept it as part of the process.

Embrace the German method: Document your failures systematically. What went wrong? What did you learn? How will you apply this knowledge next time?

Try the Scandinavian celebration: Instead of hiding your failures, share them. Connect with other entrepreneurs who understand that failure is data, not defeat.

Apply indigenous patience: Understand that mastery requires multiple failures. You are not behind schedule if you are still learning.

Try this: Write down your last three "failures," and next to each one, note what it taught you. You might be surprised by how much wisdom you've already gained.

The path from $1,200 to $32,000 wasn't a straight line. It was a series of course corrections informed by failure. Each "wrong" turn taught me something essential about the right direction.

Your failures aren't roadblocks; they're road signs. They are information on how to proceed more effectively. Because once you understand that failure isn't just normal, it's neurologically necessary, everything changes.

CHAPTER 3
Your Brain on Failure

Neuroplasticity and Mistakes:
How Failure Literally Rewires Your Brain for Success

Most people think failure just feels bad, but what if I told you it's actually making you smarter? What if every mistake or flop was literally rewiring your brain for long-term success? Science proves it, and once you understand how your brain responds to failure, you will stop avoiding it and start using it.

Every time you fail, your brain gets stronger. Failure doesn't just teach life lessons; it literally rewires your brain, strengthening neural pathways, improving cognitive flexibility, and building emotional resilience.

I wish I had known this during my years of educational conditioning. I wish someone had told me that when Ahmed got those math problems "wrong," his brain was actually building new neural pathways that would improve his problem-solving skills. I wish someone had explained that when my first Etsy shop generated only modest sales, my brain was rewiring itself for future success.

But nobody taught us this in education school. Nobody explained that failure isn't just psychologically beneficial; it's neurologically necessary.

There's a scientific concept that explains exactly how failure helps us grow, and it's called neuroplasticity.

Your Brain on Failure: The Neuroplasticity Revolution

For most of human history, scientists believed that adult brains were fixed and that once you reached maturity, your neural pathways were set in stone. This belief reinforced our educational approach: get it right the first time because your brain can't really change. The notion was often echoed in sayings like "you can't teach an old dog new tricks."

But in the 1990s, neuroscientist Dr. Michael Merzenich and his colleagues discovered something revolutionary that proved the opposite: adult brains are incredibly plastic. They can reorganize, adapt, and grow new neural connections throughout our lives. And here's the kicker: they do this most dramatically when we're challenged, when we make mistakes, when we fail.

Dr. Carol Dweck's research at Stanford University revealed that when students encounter difficult problems and make mistakes, their brains show increased activity in areas associated with learning and growth. The struggle isn't a sign that learning isn't happening; it's evidence that it is occurring at the deepest level.

When you fail at something, several incredible things happen in your brain:

Myelin Production Increases: Myelin is like insulation on electrical wiring. It's the fatty substance that wraps around neural pathways, making them stronger and faster. Research shows that struggling with challenging tasks increases myelin production by up to 200%. Your failures literally make your brain more efficient.

New Neural Pathways Form: When your usual approach doesn't work, your brain starts building alternative routes, like creating new roads when the main highway is blocked. These new pathways often become more sophisticated than the original ones, which is why people who struggle early often develop into more creative problem-solvers.

The Anterior Cingulate Cortex Activates: Think of this as your brain's personal troubleshooting department. When you encounter failure, this region lights up and begins scanning for new solutions. It's like your brain's innovation center going into overdrive.

Dopamine Pathways Strengthen: Contrary to popular belief, the most powerful dopamine release doesn't come from easy success. It comes from overcoming challenges and solving problems after repeated attempts. Your brain literally rewards you more for difficult victories than for easy wins.

The Ahmed Effect: How Mistakes Build Mastery

Remember Ahmed, the bright 10-year-old I taught in Kuwait who struggled with traditional math methods? What I didn't realize at the time was that I was witnessing neuroplasticity in action.

Every time Ahmed got a problem "wrong" using traditional methods, his brain was actually building alternative neural pathways. The weeks of struggle weren't evidence of his inadequacy; they were proof of his brain developing a more sophisticated mathematical operating system.

Dr. Jo Boaler's research at Stanford shows that students who struggle with math and make mistakes develop more robust mathematical thinking than those who get everything right immediately. The struggle creates what she calls "neural pathway diversity"—multiple ways of approaching and solving problems.

This explains why some of my most "successful" students, the ones who earned straight A's without effort, often struggled later when they faced truly challenging material. Their brains hadn't had the opportunity to build the resilience pathways that come from productive failure.

Meanwhile, students like Ahmed, who had to work harder and fail more, developed what neuroscientists call "cognitive flexibility." It is the ability to adapt their thinking when circumstances change.

The Entrepreneurial Brain: Why Business Failure Creates Business Brilliance

This neuroplasticity research completely reframes entrepreneurial failure. Every business setback you experience rewires your brain for better decision-making, more creative problem-solving, and increased resilience.

When my first Etsy shop struggled, my brain was busy:

- **Pattern Recognition:** Learning to identify what types of products customers actually wanted versus what I thought they should want.

- **Emotional Regulation:** Strengthening pathways that help manage disappointment and maintain motivation despite setbacks.

- **Adaptive Strategies:** Building mental flexibility to pivot when initial strategies fail.

- **Risk Assessment:** Improving my brain's ability to evaluate opportunities and make better decisions under uncertainty.

Dr. Martin Seligman's research on "learned optimism" shows that people who experience controlled failures can learn from and overcome them. They actually develop stronger neural pathways associated with resilience, persistence, and creative problem-solving.

The keyword is "controlled." Random, meaningless failures don't build these pathways. But failures that come from taking calculated risks, trying new approaches, and pushing beyond comfort zones? Those failures are like strength training for your brain.

The Learning Loop:
Fail → Analyze → Adapt → Apply → Repeat

That's where the Learning Loop comes in. It's a five-step process used by entrepreneurs, educators, and creators alike to turn missteps into momentum. But here's the difference: I've adapted it to fit my journey.

Because there's no one-size-fits-all path to success. What works for someone else might not fit your stage, your strengths, or your story.

Therefore, I want you to do the same. Make it work for *you*. This isn't a rigid framework; it's a rhythm. One you can return to, tweak, and reshape as you grow.

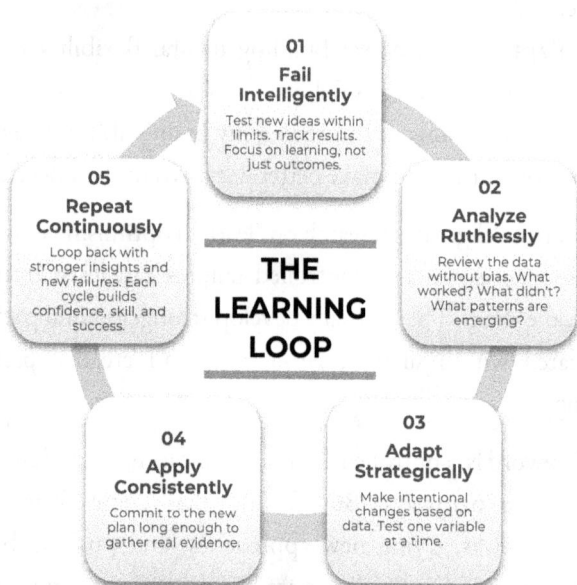

01
Fail Intelligently
Test new ideas within limits. Track results. Focus on learning, not just outcomes.

05
Repeat Continuously
Loop back with stronger insights and new failures. Each cycle builds confidence, skill, and success.

THE LEARNING LOOP

02
Analyze Ruthlessly
Review the data without bias. What worked? What didn't? What patterns are emerging?

04
Apply Consistently
Commit to the new plan long enough to gather real evidence.

03
Adapt Strategically
Make intentional changes based on data. Test one variable at a time.

Step 1: Fail (Intelligently)

Not all failures are created equally. Random, careless failures offer little learning. Intelligent failures are those that arise from testing hypotheses, pushing boundaries, and trying new approaches, and they are invaluable.

Characteristics of intelligent failures:

- **Bounded:** You identify the maximum downside before you start. Like testing a $25 ad campaign instead of a $500 one.
- **Documented:** You track what you try and what happens.
- **Intentional:** You are testing specific hypotheses rather than hoping for the best.
- **Affordable:** You can learn from them without facing devastating consequences.

When I started my second Etsy shop, I applied this principle. Instead of creating 50 products and hoping something would work, I began with 5 carefully chosen products in a specific niche. This limited my potential failure while maximizing my learning.

Step 2: Analyze (Ruthlessly)

This is where most people struggle with failure. They encounter a setback and immediately jump to trying something else without extracting valuable lessons.

The analysis framework I use:

What happened? (Facts, not emotions)

- Which products sold and which didn't?
- What was my conversion rate by traffic source?
- How did different price points perform?
- What customer feedback did I receive?

Why did it happen? (Root cause analysis)

- Was it a product, marketing, or timing issue?
- Did I target the wrong audience or the right audience with the wrong message?

- Were my assumptions about customer behavior accurate?

What does this tell me about my market? (Market intelligence)

- What do customers actually value versus what I thought they valued?
- Where do they discover new products?
- What language resonates with them?
- What problems are they trying to solve?

What would I do differently? (Actionable insights)

- Specific changes to product, pricing, positioning, or promotion
- New hypotheses to test
- Different segments to target

Tip: Create a recurring "Failure Reflection" template with these questions. Copy them into a reusable document after every setback or experiment. It will become your most valuable learning tool, turning every disappointment into actionable intelligence.

Step 3: Adapt (Strategically)

Based on your analysis, adapt your approach. This isn't about random changes; it's about strategic iteration grounded in data.

Adaptation principles:

Change one variable at a time: If you alter everything simultaneously, you won't know what caused any improvements or deteriorations.

Test opposing hypotheses: If low prices didn't work, try higher prices. If long descriptions don't convert, test shorter ones.

Build on what worked: Don't discard everything. Amplify the successful elements while addressing those that didn't perform.

Stay close to your core: Adapt tactics freely, but don't abandon your fundamental value proposition: your core customer, mission, or niche without strong evidence.

After reviewing the performance of my first shop, I noticed something important:
my holiday-themed products consistently outsold my creative templates.

At first, I thought it was just seasonal luck. But then I looked deeper.

This particular shop was designed to serve businesses in the **gift niche**, and holidays were when they made most of their money. They weren't just buying digital products; they were buying *timing*. They needed seasonal POD solutions they could resell or use during peak sales windows.

That realization helped me shift. I needed to lean more heavily into holiday-themed offers and began phasing out products that didn't serve that buying behavior.

Buyer behavior isn't fixed. What works now might shift next season. That's why you have to let your data guide you, not assumptions.

Step 4: Apply (Consistently)

Knowledge without application is worthless. This step involves implementing your adaptations consistently and for long enough to gather meaningful data.

Application principles:

Commit to the test period: Give your adaptations enough time to generate reliable data. Most marketplace algorithms require 30-60 days to optimize.

Track leading indicators: Don't just monitor sales. Keep an eye on views, likes, favorites, conversion rates, and other metrics that predict sales.

Maintain discipline: It's tempting to make constant small adjustments, but this hampers your ability to gather clean data on any single approach.

Document everything: Keep detailed records of what you are testing, why you are testing it, and the results you are obtaining.

Step 5: Repeat (Continuously)

The Learning Loop isn't a one-time process. It's a continuous cycle that becomes faster and more sophisticated over time.

Why repetition is crucial:

Compound learning: Each cycle builds on the previous ones, leading to exponential rather than linear improvement.

Faster pattern recognition: Your brain becomes more adept at identifying what works and what doesn't.

Reduced emotional resistance: Failure shifts from feeling personal to being part of data collection.

Increased risk tolerance: As you prove your ability to learn from failures, you become more willing to take bigger intelligent risks.

By my third month of using the Learning Loop, something shifted. I went from cycling through it monthly to revisiting it every single week.

I could spot problems faster, adapt more quickly, and make changes with a new sense of confidence. Not because it was easy or flashy, but because it was *grounded*. It gave me real data I could trust.

To be honest, the Learning Loop wasn't my favorite strategy at first. It felt slow. It was a little tedious. But the more I used it, the more I realized it was working.

It reminded me of what we do in education. When a student is struggling, we don't guess. We look at the data. We ask, *What is this telling us? What's missing? What can we shift to get better results?*

The Learning Loop gave me that same clarity in business.

It's not a magic formula, but it is a reliable one. Especially if you are running a storefront or trying to improve your digital products. If you lean into it, even for a short season, you'll start to see what's working, what's not, and exactly what to do next.

And that's the kind of insight most entrepreneurs skip.

Psychological Safety: Creating Environments Where Failure Breeds Innovation

Here's something critical that most entrepreneurs overlook: you can't grow through failure in an environment that punishes it. You need what Harvard Business School professor Amy

Edmondson describes as *"psychological safety"*—the belief that you can make mistakes without facing punishment or humiliation.

The Failure-Phobic Environment

Most of us come from failure-phobic environments. But this fear doesn't just appear later in life.
It's planted early, when we're still forming our sense of identity.

Somewhere between red ink and gold stars, we learned that failure was something to fear, not something to learn from. We weren't taught to separate who we are from what didn't work.

We internalized it. We silenced ourselves. We settled for "safe." Instead of building resilience, we built walls. Instead of trying again, we learned to avoid trying at all.

Over time, this conditioning becomes a quiet, invisible, and suffocating cage. And it doesn't just stop you from taking risks in business. It keeps you from showing up fully in your life.

Because a fear of failure isn't just a mindset. It became a subconscious rule we started living by: Avoid mistakes. Stay in line. Don't disappoint. And we carry that rule into every room we enter, especially the ones where we most need courage. You have probably seen it play out in every area of life:

Educational settings where mistakes led to lower grades, disappointed teachers, and parental consequences.

Corporate environments where failures resulted in poor performance reviews, missed promotions, and potential job loss.

Social environments where failures led to judgment, gossip, and exclusion.

These environments condition us to hide failures, avoid risks, and play it safe. But entrepreneurship demands the opposite: exposing failures, taking risks, and pushing boundaries.

Creating Your Own Psychological Safety

Since most external environments aren't naturally failure-friendly, we must cultivate our own psychological safety. Here's how:

Reframe failure language:

- Instead of "I failed," say "I learned."
- Instead of "This didn't work," say "This data is valuable."
- Instead of "I'm not good at this," say "I'm still learning, and every step is progress."

Set learning goals instead of performance goals:

- Performance goal: "Make $5,000 this month."
- Learning goal: "Test three different pricing strategies this month."

Celebrate intelligent failures:

- Maintain a "failure journal" documenting each setback, including the failure itself, what you tried, what happened, how you felt, and what you learned. It serves as a space for both data and emotional honesty.
- Share your failures with other entrepreneurs who recognize their value.

- Reward yourself for taking calculated risks, regardless of the outcome.

Create failure budgets:

- Allocate funds specifically for experiments that might not succeed.
- Limit the downside of any single test so failure can't devastate you.
- Consider this an investment in R&D (Research and Development), not gambling.

Building a Failure-Friendly Business

Your business must be designed for intelligent failure:

Start small and iterate: Launch minimal viable products to quickly and affordably test hypotheses. What this entails varies by expertise. If you are a teacher, perhaps it's a single lesson plan template rather than a full curriculum. If you are a designer, it might be one social media template instead of an entire brand package. If you are a consultant, consider offering a one-hour workshop instead of a six-month program.

Build feedback loops: Establish systems that provide rapid, honest feedback on what works and what doesn't.

Diversify your tests: Avoid relying on a single product or strategy. Conduct multiple small experiments simultaneously.

Plan for pivots: Design your business model to be flexible enough to adapt based on your learnings.

The Support System Factor

One major challenge for entrepreneurs from traditional backgrounds (teachers, corporate employees, etc.) is that existing support systems often fail to recognize the value of failure.

These aren't merely personal doubts; they're cultural scripts we have internalized:

- "Maybe you should just get a regular job."
- "When are you going to start making real money?"
- "This seems too risky."
- "Why don't you just play it safe?"

Building a failure-friendly support system:

Find other entrepreneurs who understand that failure is part of the process. Online communities, local meetups, and entrepreneurship groups can provide this support.

Educate your family about your approach. Share articles, books, or examples of successful entrepreneurs who turned failures into stepping stones.

Work with mentors who have navigated the entrepreneurial journey themselves and can normalize its ups and downs.

Consider professional support from business coaches or therapists who specialize in entrepreneurial challenges.

The framing of these responses as "cultural scripts we have absorbed" is effective. It positions them as societal programming rather than personal attacks, fostering empowerment for readers facing similar situations. This perspective helps them realize their resistance isn't personal; it's a result of cultural conditioning that can be overcome.

Research Review:
Studies Proving Failure's Role in Long-Term Success

The link between failure and success isn't just theoretical; it's scientifically validated. Here are some compelling research findings that support the fail-forward approach.

The Harvard Business School Study

Professors Francesca Gino and Bradley Staats conducted an intriguing study involving over 1,500 entrepreneurs. They found that those who had faced at least one significant business failure were notably more successful across various metrics.

The Learning from Failure Research

Dr. Kathryn Dekas at Google led an extensive study of over 2,000 projects within the company. The findings revealed that teams experiencing early, small failures developed superior learning capabilities that benefited them throughout the project lifecycle.

Research Summary

Metric	Harvard Study (Entrepreneurs)	Google Study (Teams)
Success Rate	30% more likely to succeed	70% more likely to achieve objectives
Problem-Solving	25% more creative	60% faster at identifying solutions

Innovation	40% better at spotting opportunities	45% more innovative solutions
Risk Assessment	50% more realistic planning	80% better at future risk evaluation

The Bottom Line: Entrepreneurs with failure experience are 30-80% more successful across every relevant metric—creativity, opportunity recognition, problem-solving speed, and overall success rates. Failure isn't just beneficial; it's scientifically proven to be essential for peak performance.

The Resilience Development Study

Dr. Ann Masten's longitudinal research tracked 3,000 individuals over 20 years, examining their responses to various challenges and failures. The study revealed that those who encountered moderate challenges early in their careers developed what she terms "ordinary magic"—exceptional resilience that served them throughout their lives.

Key findings:

- Individuals who faced no significant challenges struggled when they eventually encountered difficulties.
- Those who faced moderate, manageable challenges developed superior coping mechanisms.
- The most successful individuals had experienced and overcome multiple failures before age 30.
- Early failure experience was a better predictor of long-term success than early success.

The Neuroscience of Productive Failure

Dr. Jason Moser's research at Michigan State University employed EEG technology to study brain activity during learning. His team discovered that when individuals made mistakes and corrected them, their brains exhibited significantly increased activity in areas associated with:

- Enhanced attention and focus
- Improved memory consolidation
- Increased cognitive flexibility
- Stronger pattern recognition

Most importantly, this heightened brain activity persisted for hours after the failure experience, indicating that failure creates a learning state that benefits all subsequent activities.

The Entrepreneurial Failure Database

The Kauffman Foundation maintains the world's largest database of entrepreneurial ventures, tracking over 50,000 businesses over multiple decades. Their analysis reveals:

- First-time entrepreneurs: 18% success rate
- Second-time entrepreneurs (after failure): 20% success rate
- Third-time entrepreneurs (after two failures): 25% success rate
- Fourth-time entrepreneurs (after three failures): 30% success rate

The pattern is clear: each failure increases the likelihood of future success, up to a point. The database indicates that entrepreneurs who have failed multiple times develop superior skills in:

- Market validation
- Customer development
- Resource management
- Team building
- Risk assessment

The Meta-Analysis of Failure Studies

Dr. Dean Shepherd at Indiana University conducted a meta-analysis of 47 studies on entrepreneurial failure, involving over 15,000 entrepreneurs across 23 countries. The comprehensive analysis revealed:

Failure experience strongly correlates with:

- **Improved decision-making** under uncertainty
- **Enhanced opportunity recognition** abilities
- **Better resource allocation** skills
- **Increased emotional resilience**
- **Superior learning orientation**

The study also identified the optimal "failure dose": entrepreneurs who experienced 2-4 significant failures showed the best outcomes. Those with no failures lacked resilience, while those with more than 5 failures sometimes developed learned helplessness.

The Biological Basis of Failure Learning

Dr. Mauricio Delgado's neuroscience research at Rutgers University used fMRI scans to study brain responses to failure and success. The results were striking:

During failure experiences:

- The anterior cingulate cortex (error detection) exhibited 300% increased activity.
- The prefrontal cortex (planning and strategy) remained highly active for 45 minutes after failure.
- Dopamine pathways showed sustained activation, contrary to expectations.

During easy success experiences:

- Brain activity quickly returned to baseline.
- Learning-associated regions showed minimal activation.
- Long-term memory formation was significantly reduced.

The conclusion: our brains are literally designed to learn more from failure than from success.

The Compound Effect: How Small Failures Create Massive Breakthroughs

Individual failures might feel small. Forgettable, even. But when you learn from them and keep going, they start to stack. They multiply. And over time, they create exponential growth, the kind of transformation that feels sudden from the outside but is built brick by brick behind the scenes.

Understanding Compound Learning

Just like compound interest turns small financial deposits into serious wealth, compound learning turns small mistakes into deep expertise. The formula is simple but powerful:

Small Failure + Learning (Insight) + Action = Marginal Improvement

Marginal Improvement × Time × Repetition = Breakthrough Success

Most people give up in the middle of this process, right when the improvements are still small and the results feel slow. But that's where the real shift begins.

Breakthroughs don't come from giant leaps. They come from tiny, compounding steps that most people don't have the patience to repeat. It's not about luck or going viral. It's about choosing to keep showing up: learning, adjusting, and repeating long enough for those small improvements to stack.

My Personal Compound Effect Journey

Let me show you how this played out in my own business:

Month 1-3 (First Etsy Shop):

- Small failure: Posted products randomly without market research.
- Learning: Customers seek solutions to specific problems, not just "pretty things."
- Application: Researched trending keywords and customer pain points.
- Result: 5% improvement in click-through rates.

Month 4-6:

- Small failure: Products weren't optimized for Etsy's search algorithm.
- Learning: SEO principles apply to Etsy just like they do to Google.
- Application: Revised all product titles and descriptions using keyword research.
- Result: 15% improvement in search visibility.

Month 7-9:

- Small failure: Pricing was too low, attracting customers who undervalued the products.
- Learning: Price communicates value just as effectively as product descriptions.
- Application: Increased prices by 20% and enhanced product presentation.
- Result: 25% improvement in profit margins and customer satisfaction.

Month 10-12:

- Small failure: Tried to compete on price, but overseas sellers were undercutting the market and devaluing the products.
- Learning: Competing on price is a losing game. Standing out with custom and high-value offers are what attracts loyal buyers.
- Application: Shifted focus to personalized and niche-specific designs based on customer needs instead of mass-market trends.
- Result: Saw a 20% increase in conversion rates across my shops by offering products that felt tailored and premium.

Each of these failures felt frustrating in that moment. But in hindsight, they were essential. Each one gave me insight. Each one pushed me to adapt. And together, those small 5%–25% improvements added up to a business I could be proud of.

The Breakthrough Threshold

As I kept learning and refining, I reached what's often called the Breakthrough Threshold—not the moment when everything suddenly exploded, but the moment when everything finally made sense.

I didn't just have more sales. I had clarity.

By this point, I had spent over a year failing forward and building real expertise in:

- Market research
- Customer psychology
- SEO optimization
- Pricing strategy
- Product positioning
- Customer experience

And here's what I realized: I had mastered the Etsy game. I had created multiple successful shops. I had even helped others build shops that became Star Sellers. But more importantly, I had learned how to read the data, solve real problems, and create products with purpose.

And that clarity made one thing obvious: I couldn't keep playing small by building on someone else's platform. I needed to build something of my own—outside of Etsy's limitations, algorithms, and shifting rules.

That's when I started shifting my energy into platforms I could control—my own Shopify store, my own email list, my own brand. Because success isn't just about getting more traffic. It's about owning the path forward.

Without those 12+ months of testing, failing, and iterating, I wouldn't have known what to build. But because I stayed with the process, I didn't just grow—I grew with intention. And that made all the difference.

The Three Stages of Compound Learning

Compound learning doesn't happen in a flash—it unfolds in phases. Each one tests a different part of you: your patience, your problem-solving, your identity. But each one also builds a layer of strength, clarity, and resilience you can't get any other way.

Let's break down what each stage looks and feels like.

Stage 1: Accumulation (Months 1-6)

This is the **foundation phase**. You're putting in work, but the results feel invisible.

- **What's happening:** You're making your first attempts—launching products, trying platforms, testing ideas. Most of them won't work the way you hoped.
- **How it feels:** Frustrating, slow, and personal. Every failure feels like proof that you're not good enough. You question whether you're even cut out for this.
- **What to remember:** You're not behind—you're in training. You're gathering raw material for your breakthrough, even if it feels like loss right now.

Think of it like planting seeds. The work is underground. No visible results—but roots are forming.

Stage 2: Acceleration (Months 7-18)

This is the **refinement phase.** Your data starts working *for* you.

- **What's happening:** You've made enough mistakes to start seeing patterns. You're no longer guessing—you're iterating based on insight.
- **How it feels:** Smoother. Encouraging. Still challenging—but now the struggle has structure. You can predict outcomes better. You're not chasing every idea—you're focused.
- **What to remember:** This is where many people settle. But you're not here just to grow. You're here to master.

Think of it like learning to drive. At first, you're hyper-aware of everything. Then suddenly, your foot finds the gas, and you're cruising.

Stage 3: Breakthrough (Months 19+)

This is the **ownership phase**. You're no longer reacting—you're leading.

- **What's happening:** You know your audience. You've built trust. You don't chase trends—you create them. Your systems work even when you're resting.
- **How it feels:** Grounded. Clear. Challenging but no longer chaotic. You trust yourself. Your confidence isn't loud; it's earned.

- **What to remember:** This is the payoff of every unseen effort you made before. But it's also the beginning of *new levels* of growth.

Think of it like compound interest. You've been investing for months now, and the returns multiply without needing twice the effort.

The Three Stages of Compound Learning. Compound learning doesn't happen in a flash; it unfolds in phases. Each one tests a different part of you: your patience, your problem-solving, your identity. But each one also builds a layer of strength, clarity, and resilience you can't get any other way.

Note: These timelines are just examples, not rules. Some people stay in Stage 1 longer. Others loop between phases. That's normal. The goal isn't to "hurry up and reach breakthrough." It's to stay in the game long enough for the process to work.

Growth doesn't follow a calendar. It follows your *willingness to keep learning*.

Designing for Compound Learning

Compound growth isn't just something you *experience*—it's something you can design for. Here's how to structure your work for sustainable learning:

- **Document everything:** Track what you try, what happens, and what you learn. This turns chaos into clarity.
- **Look for patterns:** Review your notes regularly. Don't just move on—mine the insight.
- **Stack lessons:** Let each experience inform the next. Never start from scratch if you've already paid for the lesson.

- **Raise the bar slowly:** Once you've mastered the basics, take on more complexity intentionally.
- **Celebrate forward motion:** Progress may feel invisible in the day-to-day, but it stacks fast over time.

Remember: You're not falling behind when you fail. You're *building ahead*. Each failure is a deposit into your future capability account.

The Network Effect of Learning

Here's something you might not expect: as your learning compounds, so does your influence. People start to notice. This is called the *network effect of learning*—where growth multiplies not just through effort, but through connection, collaboration, and shared trust.

Why this happens:

- People are drawn to those who treat failure as feedback
- Your questions become deeper and attract better answers
- Sharing your process builds trust and attracts aligned partners
- Your resilience makes you a magnetic leader

I began to see this around Month 20. One company reached out and paid me $1,000 to support a project they were launching. Another reached out shortly after with an invitation to collaborate on a separate initiative. These weren't viral moments or flashy wins, just quiet proof that the foundation I had built was starting to echo back.

I wasn't just learning from my own experience anymore. I was learning through theirs, gaining insights, asking better questions, and expanding my perspective. That's the beauty of the network effect. Once you start compounding progress, the learning doesn't just get faster; it comes from every direction.

The Science Behind Compound Learning

This isn't just a nice concept; it's backed by brain science. Each failure provides the feedback necessary for the next level of challenge.

- Dr. Anders Ericsson's research on deliberate practice shows that expertise develops through repeated cycles of:

  1. Attempting challenging tasks.
  2. Receiving feedback (often through failure).
  3. Adjusting approach based on feedback.
  4. Attempting progressively more challenging tasks.

- Dr. Barbara Oakley's research adds that your brain processes these lessons *between* the work. That's why growth can feel slow in the moment—but dramatic in hindsight. Your brain is wiring itself during the quiet.

Let the Data Lead You

The greatest breakthrough in my business wasn't a product. It was a shift in perspective.

I realized that if I paid attention to the data—my results, my failures, my feedback—it would always show me what to do next.

And that's the key, not just in business, but in life. If you pay attention, the data will always show you something. It will tell you when it's time to pivot, when it's time to stretch, when it's time to stop guessing and start aligning. You won't always know the full plan, but you will always have enough evidence to take the next right step.

Business isn't about picking the "perfect" path on Day 1. It's about moving forward, listening to what the journey is teaching you, and letting that feedback shape what comes next. You may start in someone else's space and end up building your own brand. You may begin selling one product and end up building a movement.

That's the beauty of this process—it evolves as *you* evolve.

PART II

THE AWAKENING

CHAPTER 4

The $32K Education
I Didn't Know I Was Paying For

It's December 31, 2022, and I'm at my kitchen table, frantically setting up my first Etsy shop at 11:47 PM. YouTube plays in the background, but that screen seems to watch me more than I watch it. I can hear the refrigerator's soft hum and the neighbor's dog barking at distant fireworks. My three teenagers are in their rooms upstairs (it's winter break, so who knows if they're actually sleeping), my husband is asleep (he goes to bed early), and I'm about to make the most educational decision of my entrepreneurial journey.

I'm about to start my first Etsy shop.

It felt almost silly to launch a business at the very last moment of the year, as if I needed the symbolic weight of a fresh calendar to give me permission to try something again. But that's exactly what I needed: a clean slate, a new beginning, a moment when "this is the year I finally do something for myself" felt possible rather than selfish.

As I typed in my shop name, I chewed my nails and whispered to myself, "Okay... here we go again." I was nervous, unsure of what to name it, what colors to pick, how I'd stand out, or how long it might take to make a sale. But beneath all that was the real fear: *"What if I'm just setting myself up for another disappointment?"*

But then I reminded myself of something even louder than the fear: I already had proof. The templates I was selling now, I had actually used in my print-on-demand business. And they sold. This wasn't a shot in the dark. This was a calculated step forward.

And honestly? Even if it didn't go viral, I wouldn't lose. And win or not, this was another step in the right direction.

At 11:58 PM, I uploaded my first product: a template set of message cards for print-on-demand business owners. It wasn't fancy; it was a product I had used when my POD business didn't take off.

At 11:59 PM, I published my shop.

At 12:00 AM on January 1, 2023, I officially became an entrepreneur—again.

As I stared at my first listing go live, I couldn't help but think back.

This wasn't my first attempt at entrepreneurship. I'd tried many ventures before—different online projects, side hustles, experiments. They all taught me something, even if they didn't take off the way I hoped.

The discouragement wasn't from the effort. It was from the outcome. I had income goals in mind, and when I didn't hit them, I started to wonder: *Maybe that wasn't the right thing. Maybe I just haven't found it yet.*

But one thing I never questioned was that I was meant for this. I've always known I was an entrepreneur. I just hadn't found my lane.

I had no idea I was about to begin the most expensive education of my life—paid not just in money, but in time, emotional energy, and the unraveling of everything I thought I knew about success and failure.

The Setup: What I Thought I Knew

Walking into entrepreneurship with a teacher's mindset is like attending a music festival expecting a classical symphony. All your training tells you there should be sheet music, a conductor, and a predetermined outcome. Instead, you get improvisation, collaboration, and beautiful chaos. It's messy, instinct-driven, and utterly disorienting to someone accustomed to clear rubrics.

Here's what I thought I knew about business:

Work hard, get results. In teaching, effort usually correlates with outcomes. Spend extra time prepping a lesson? Your students generally perform better. I assumed business worked the same way. (It doesn't.)

Follow the rules, succeed. Education is built on systems: clear procedures, best practices, and step-by-step guidance. There's a "right" way to write a lesson plan, manage a classroom, or evaluate student work. I figured business had a similar structure: learn the rules, get the reward.

(It doesn't.)

Quality equals demand. As a teacher, thoughtful, well-designed lessons always earned better engagement. So, I assumed that high-quality digital products would automatically attract buyers. (They didn't.)

Time invested equals value created. In the classroom, the more time something takes to create, the more valuable it tends to be. That didn't translate either. Some of my most time-consuming products barely sold.

One-size-fits-all solutions work. Standardization is the backbone of the education system. Build something that helps "most" people, and it usually works. But business isn't built on average; it's built on specificity.

Every one of these assumptions was about to be shattered. Thank goodness, because those beliefs were what kept me stuck in mediocrity.

The Reality Check: Month One

My first sale came on January 10th: $3.50 for a set of Valentine message cards. I was heading to the grocery store with my family when the notification popped up on my phone. I literally screamed in the parking lot. My kids looked at me like I'd lost my mind. "I made my first sale!" I shouted, dancing around like I'd won the lottery.

Three dollars and fifty cents. Less than a fancy coffee. But at that moment, it felt like proof that this was possible, that I wasn't completely delusional, and that maybe I could actually build something. I knew the designs were solid since I had made sales with those same templates when I sold POD jewelry, but seeing them work in this new context felt like validation.

By the end of January, I had made exactly $68.62 in revenue.

To put this in perspective: I was working 1-3 hours every evening after my teaching job, plus 4-6 hours on weekends. That's roughly 50 hours of work for $68.62. If I'd gotten a part-time job at minimum wage, I would have made over $350.

But here's what I was really learning in those 50 hours:

Customer psychology: People buy solutions to problems, not products because they're pretty.

Platform dynamics: Etsy has an algorithm that doesn't care how much time you spent creating something.

Market research: What you think people want and what they actually want are often completely different.

Competition analysis: There are thousands of other sellers, and most of them know things you don't.

SEO fundamentals: Search engine optimization isn't just for websites; it's crucial for marketplace success.

I didn't realize I was learning these things at the time. I just knew I was failing to make the money I'd dreamed about. But failure, as I now understand, is education in disguise.

The Grind: Months Two Through Six

February through July 2023 was what I now call "The Grind," and if you are starting out, you'll likely have your own version of these months. Here's what mine looked like:

- **February**: $20.49 — The dreaded backslide that makes you question everything.
- **March**: $76.03 — Encouraging growth that feels like breakthrough.
- **April**: $34.61 — Reality check that progress isn't always linear.
- **May**: $24.74 — The humbling month that tests your commitment.
- **June**: $14.55 — Rock bottom that either breaks you or builds resilience.
- **July**: $21.60 — Slight improvement that offers a glimmer of hope.
- **August**: $122 — Real progress that validates the process.

Looking back, these numbers reflect more than just the typical entrepreneurial rollercoaster. They show someone treating their business like a hobby. I was working sporadically, when I felt like it, without the consistency and strategic focus that real business growth requires. Most new entrepreneurs experience similar emotional and financial ups and downs, but these results also reveal the difference between dabbling and committing.

What these numbers don't show is the emotional rollercoaster I was riding. Every uptick felt like validation. Every downturn felt like evidence that I wasn't cut out for this. I was still operating with a teacher's mindset: consistent effort should produce consistent results.

My biggest mistake during this period was falling into what many entrepreneurs now refer to as "The Product Creation Trap"— spending hours perfecting products that were never validated and wondering why they didn't sell.

I experienced both sides of this trap. First, I was targeting an impossibly small niche: message cards for print-on-demand business owners. At the time, there were probably only 50 to 100 people searching for these each month on Etsy, and I wasn't the only seller creating them.

Second, I was obsessing over perfection instead of focusing on volume or market testing. I'd spend entire days tweaking display images and refining designs, convincing myself this was "real work." In reality, I was using perfectionism as an excuse to avoid the scarier task of finding out what customers actually wanted.

The result? Lots of beautiful products that almost nobody was looking for, created at a pace so slow that even if there had been demand, I couldn't have capitalized on it.

The SEO Awakening

I knew I could make some income, but I also knew this shop wasn't going to grow through guesswork and message cards alone. I needed direction. I needed someone who had walked the path before me. So, I hired someone on Etsy to do a full shop audit.

The feedback was sobering—but exactly what I needed. I learned I wasn't using all my tags. My titles were repetitive. My keywords were too similar. My descriptions lacked clarity. And my mockups? They needed some serious TLC.

The audit came with a clear list of action steps: Fix your SEO. Clean up your listings. Add more products. I tried. But instead of building, I got stuck again, browsing other shops, obsessing over aesthetics, sitting at the screen far more than I was taking action.

Still, by the end of the year, my shop had generated over $1,200, even after hiring an expert twice. That told me something: progress happens when you stop trying to be perfect and start making moves.

That was one of the most important lessons I've ever learned:

Success doesn't come from perfect plans. It comes from consistent **action.** I spent so many hours trying to "get it right" before I let it be seen, but that's like writing a flawless lesson plan and never teaching the class.

The $1,200 Lesson: Why My First Year "Failed" (and Why It Was Perfect)

By January 1, 2024, one full year after launching my Etsy shop, I had made exactly $1,247.89.

A year of effort. A little over $100 a month. On paper, that looked like failure. By any reasonable measure, this appeared to be a failure. Yes, I could have earned more working hourly jobs or tutoring students with my teaching skills. But this venture was about more than income; it was an investment in a skill set that no hourly job could provide.

Here's what that $1,247.89 actually bought me:

Market Research Worth Thousands

I tested 47 different product concepts across multiple niches, gaining insights into which products resonated with customers and which ones flopped. I gathered data on:

- **Seasonal trends:** What sold during back-to-school, holidays, and New Year's resolution season.
- **Price sensitivity:** How customers reacted to $2.99 vs. $7.99 vs. $15.99 products.
- **Format preferences:** PDFs vs. editable files vs. printables vs. digital templates.
- **Niche performance:** Non-themed message cards outsold creative templates 3:1.
- **Customer behavior:** People bought solutions to immediate problems—not abstract improvements.

This market research would have cost tens of thousands of dollars if I'd hired a consulting firm. Instead, I acquired it by navigating real customer interactions.

Platform Mastery Worth More

I became fluent in Etsy's algorithm, SEO requirements, customer psychology, and competitive landscape. I learned:

- **How Etsy's search algorithm prioritized products.**
- **Which keywords actually drove traffic versus those that sounded appealing.**

- **How to optimize product photos for mobile browsing.**
- **What compelled customers to click "add to cart" instead of continuing to browse.**
- **How to handle customer service issues professionally.**

This mastery of the platform couldn't be gleaned from courses or books; it could only be earned through countless interactions with real customers in a genuine marketplace. If you're willing to stay in the arena, the platform will teach you everything you need to know. But only if you stop treating every dip in sales like a dead end.

Emotional Resilience Worth Everything

Most importantly, I developed entrepreneurial emotional resilience. I endured:

- **The crushing disappointment** of products I loved but customers ignored.
- **The confusion** of sales that defied logic.
- **The frustration** of hard work yielding minimal results.
- **The self-doubt** whispering, "maybe you are not cut out for this."
- **The comparison trap** of seeing other sellers' highlight reels.

This emotional education was priceless. I proved to myself that I could face uncertainty, disappointment, and slow progress—and still keep showing up. I learned to find motivation in learning rather than merely in earning.

Systems and Processes Worth Scaling

Throughout the year, I developed systems for:

- **Simple product creation** workflows I could repeat and scale.
- **Keyword research** that uncovered what buyers were already searching for.
- **Customer communication** that built trust and loyalty.
- **Inventory management** that prevented overselling digital products.
- **Financial tracking** that showed what was working, not just what was selling.

These systems weren't glamorous, but they formed the foundation for future growth.

Network and Knowledge Worth Connecting

I connected with other Etsy sellers, joined entrepreneur groups, and learned from those already successful. This network became invaluable for:

- **Troubleshooting problems** I couldn't solve alone.
- **Sharing resources** and opportunities.
- **Providing accountability** during challenging times.
- **Celebrating wins** with individuals who understood the journey.

That first year didn't launch me to success; it *equipped* me for it. And the same can be true for you. Your first $100 or your first "flop" might be the most valuable investment you'll ever make.

The Perfect Failure Formula

Looking back, I realize my first year was not a failure but a perfectly calibrated learning experience. It was:

Challenging enough to teach me valuable lessons but **not devastating enough** to destroy my confidence.

Profitable enough to prove the concept's viability but **not profitable enough** to make me complacent.

Frustrating enough to motivate change but **not frustrating enough** to make me quit.

Slow enough to build strong foundations but **not slow enough** to bore me into giving up.

Had I made $10,000 in my first year, I might have assumed I had figured everything out and lost the drive to learn and grow. If I had made $0, I might have concluded that online business was not for me.

But $1,247.89? That was just enough to prove success was possible while highlighting how much I still had to learn.

February 2024:
The Decision That Changed Everything

Somewhere in the middle of February 2024, I made a quiet promise to myself, a decision that shifted everything.

I was sitting at my desk during lunch, eating a sad desk salad and scrolling through my Etsy stats. I felt disheartened. January had been disappointing. My momentum was stalling. I was tired of the feast-or-famine cycle. Exhausted from working so hard for modest results, I felt like I was on the edge of giving up.

Instead of quitting, I made a different choice. I decided to get serious. I was going to show up like this is my real job because it is. That decision to treat this like a business, not a hobby, was the line in the sand. And everything changed after that.

The Mindset Shift

I had made a quiet but firm decision: I wanted a fresh start. My first Etsy shop had brought in steady income. It wasn't wildly successful, but it was working, and I was proud of what I had built. But the products in that shop were designed for a very specific audience. And the direction I wanted to grow in? It didn't match.

I was ready to pivot. The more I learned, the more I felt drawn to the world of digital products for business owners. Templates. Planners. Resources that could help other entrepreneurs save time and grow. But those offers didn't belong in my first shop. It didn't make sense to try to blend the two.

So, I started over—with a new shop, a new niche, and a different kind of confidence. This time, I wasn't creating from scratch; I was creating from experience.

I had already learned the basics: how Etsy's algorithm worked, how to design listings, how to fulfill orders, and how to handle customer messages. Now I wanted to take what I had learned and apply it to something that felt more aligned with my long-term vision.

But starting over didn't mean everything clicked right away. I still faced new challenges. Some days felt like I was failing all over again. The difference? This time, I didn't run. I didn't disappear. I reminded myself that this was a business, not a side project or a test.

Even though I didn't start tracking everything right away, I knew this: If I wanted different results, I had to show up differently. That shift in thinking didn't change my circumstances overnight. But it changed me. And that changed everything else.

The Strategy Overhaul

Once I committed to treating this like a business, things started to shift—not all at once, but decision by decision.

I stopped doing things the scattered way I had before. No more creating random products, hoping something would stick. No more designing for "everyone who needs to get organized." That lack of focus had been draining my energy and clouding my progress.

This time, I got intentional. I chose a clear niche: busy moms and women who wanted to start online businesses. Not because I thought it would be easy but because I knew her. I was her.

I started paying attention to what was trending and, more importantly, what was actually selling. I learned how to build around demand, not just ideas.

My branding became more consistent. I stopped switching styles every week. I picked colors, visuals, and language that actually spoke to my audience, and I stuck with it.

At first, I completely avoided content marketing. I didn't know where to start, and I was already overwhelmed. So, I leaned hard on Etsy SEO—trying to make the most of the algorithm. It wasn't perfect, but it taught me a lot about how people search, click, and decide.

Most importantly, I stopped guessing what people wanted. I started studying it. What were they actually buying? What patterns could I spot? What problems kept showing up that I could help solve? That's when I began building a business with strategy, not just hope.

When you start treating your effort like strategy, not survival, everything changes.

The Learning Acceleration

The biggest shift I made wasn't tactical—it was how I approached learning. Instead of slowly piecing things together through trial and error, I chose to accelerate the process. I joined masterminds, bought courses, and hired mentors. It was an investment, yes—but one I knew I couldn't afford *not* to make.

Every month I spent stuck in a problem someone else had already solved was time I couldn't get back. My time was more valuable than my money. And once I accepted that, things started moving faster.

I didn't need more free tips. I needed more focused direction. And I finally gave myself permission to receive it.

Multiple Shop Madness:
How Spreading Myself Thin Taught Me Focus

I didn't fail because I wasn't trying. I failed because I was trying everything at once. What I thought was hustle was really just avoidance dressed up in ambition.

In less than two years, I opened five Etsy shops. I told myself I was building multiple streams of income. And technically, it was working; I was making money and getting sales. But because I wasn't tracking anything consistently, I couldn't see the growth clearly. Without systems in place, even income started to feel like lack.

I was building something real, but I didn't feel it. I didn't see the progress. I didn't believe it was working. I kept moving. I opened new shops. I jumped to the next idea. Not because the last one had failed, but because I didn't know how to tell that it hadn't.

Here's how that lack of focus played out across five different shops:

- **Shop 1 (January 2023):** I launched with POD message cards. To keep my Star Seller badge, I kept adding random products. No niche. No direction. Just posting and praying.
- **Shop 2 (February 2024):** This was supposed to be the focused shop—centered around digital products for business owners. In hindsight, this should have been my only shop. But I didn't protect it like it mattered most.
- **Shop 3 (May 2024):** When Shop 2 got stuck in "vacation mode" and traffic tanked, I panicked. I feared Etsy would shut it down completely, so I spun up a backup. It focused

on similar digital products, but running both shops pulled me in too many directions.

- **Shop 4 (July 2024):** I moved my original POD message cards here and then layered in printable wall art and sublimation designs—because apparently, three shops weren't enough chaos.
- **Shop 5 (October 2024):** This was my "creator identity" shop. I wanted a space to showcase my original, handcrafted work, something that felt more personal. But timing-wise? It was the worst possible moment to start over again.

Writing it all out feels chaotic. Living it was even more so.

The result? I was doing the exact opposite of what every successful entrepreneur preaches: **focus on one thing until it works**.

Instead, I was splitting my time between five different shops, five different audiences, and five completely different content strategies, all while working full-time, raising a family, and trying to take care of myself.

Yes, some of the shops made sales. But imagine what might have happened if I had poured all that energy into just one. Instead of building momentum, I was constantly switching gears, patching holes, and reacting to problems instead of planning for growth.

Trying to be everywhere kept me from being effective anywhere. Focus changed everything. Once I stopped trying to do it all, real progress began. I had all the right intentions—clearer offers, better products, a stronger mindset. But without clarity and tracking, those intentions still led me straight into chaos.

The Shiny Object Syndrome

Just when one of my shops finally started gaining traction— steady growth, repeat customers, a clear direction—I made a decision that derailed everything.

Instead of doubling down on what was working, I got distracted.

It sounded smart at the time: diversify, capture new audiences, create multiple income streams. I even hired a couple of coaches to help me manage the chaos. But the truth? I wasn't expanding. I was escaping. I wasn't scaling; I was splintering.

And that decision cost me more than just time. It kept me stuck in a cycle of overthinking, starting over, and spreading myself thin—all while telling myself I was "doing the work."

The Reality of Divided Attention

Here's what happened: I started noticing patterns across different shops. I thought, *"If this item was in that shop, maybe it would sell better."* So, I moved products around. I shifted strategies. I rearranged everything.

Sometimes it worked. Most of the time, it didn't. Instead of nurturing what was already gaining momentum, I fractured my energy. I turned one growing business into multiple scattered experiments.

And while I was technically still making sales, the potential was nowhere near what it could have been because I was never giving one thing my full attention. The harsh truth? You can't multiply what you refuse to master.

Had I focused, refined, and committed to the shop that was already working, I believe the outcome would have been dramatically different. Instead, I spent months caught in a loop of "almost there," without ever getting past the starting line.

The 5 Focus Commandments I Learned the Hard Way

This chaotic season taught me several lessons I now treat as non-negotiable. These aren't just productivity tips; they're focus commandments I live by.

Commandment #1: Your attention is your most limited resource.

I only had 2–3 hours a night to work on my business. When I divided that time between five different shops, each got less than an hour. And an hour a day isn't enough to build anything sustainable. Attention is like sunlight; you can scatter it across a field, or you can focus it on one plant and watch it grow.

Commandment #2: You can't shortcut market mastery.

I was selling eBooks, social media templates, wedding designs, and more, all at the same time. Each product spoke to a different audience, with different problems, platforms, and expectations. I wasn't mastering any of them. I was stuck at the surface level, learning just enough to stay overwhelmed.

Commandment #3: Brand equity takes time and consistency to build.

My original shop had momentum because I showed up for it. Over time, customers began to trust my quality, recognize my design style, and return for more. But every time I opened a new shop, I started from zero—no reviews, no repeat buyers, no trust. Brand equity isn't instant. It's earned through repetition.

Commandment #4: Systems don't automatically scale across markets.

The strategies that worked beautifully for selling eBooks didn't work at all for wedding templates. I had to relearn keyword research, rewrite customer messaging, and rethink my visual branding. I thought I was scaling. But really, I was just multiplying my workload.

Commandment #5: Success requires depth, not width.

I was trying to be everything to everyone. And instead of becoming known for one powerful product line or niche, I became a generalist—spread thin and difficult to remember. The breakthrough came when I chose to go deep: one audience, one core product type, and one clear message.

The Overwhelm Reality

By August, I felt overwhelmed. I was posting maybe once a week, and some shops received no attention at all. I worked longer hours but felt like I accomplished little. Many products remained incomplete in my drafts. By the time I finally posted them, the trend was already declining. The drop in sales directly resulted from the confusion I had created.

I felt like a failure. I couldn't keep up with custom orders and had to decline some. I stopped seeking trending items; I would jump in when I thought something was trending, only to find it had peaked six months earlier. It was a challenging time that affected every aspect of my life.

I was so drained I stopped meal prepping, barely slept, gained a pant size or two, and completely avoided my stats. Your business and your personal life always mirror each other. And mine were both out of sync. It felt like drowning in slow motion.

To make matters worse, the new school year began, and I had to return to teaching full-time, adding more responsibilities to an already overwhelming situation.

The Non-Shutdown Decision

I wish I had shut down the extra shops. That would have been the wiser move. But instead of closing them, I tried to keep them all afloat; I just stopped working in them consistently. Hoping to ease the pressure, I hired my teenagers to help.

They assisted with uploading listings, creating mockups, and occasionally answering customer questions, all under my supervision. I thought bringing them in would solve the problem.

And in many ways, it was a blessing. Having my kids work in the business gave us more time together, and truthfully, their designs often looked better than mine. The issue wasn't their work—it was the sheer weight of managing five shops.

I spent so much time creating tasks for them, explaining my systems, and double-checking everything that I barely made progress. Even with help, I was still doing most of the work—just now with extra steps, extra oversight, and a whole lot more mental load.

We were all doing the work, but with so many moving pieces, we couldn't move the needle.

The Fresh Start

Just when I thought I'd sworn off starting over, I circled back to Shop 1.

It sounds counterintuitive, I know. But this time was different; I wasn't guessing anymore. I applied everything I'd learned from my failed attempts: stronger SEO, better branding, clearer product messaging. I carved out a niche rooted in personal growth and women's empowerment, offering everything from eBooks to mugs and tees. I hired a coach to help me gain more clarity.

And for the first time in a long time, it worked. Daily sales. Glowing reviews. Repeat customers. I felt something I hadn't felt in a while: momentum. But just like that, a new truth started to stir, one I hadn't fully faced until now.

The Education Disconnect

We spend so much time learning skills that aren't beneficial in the real world.
I have never used the Pythagorean theorem, not once since leaving school.

But I wish someone had taught me how to sell, how to handle rejection, and how to manage money.
Students need to understand how it feels when a sale flops and how to get back up when it does. These are life skills—not electives.

Yet our education system leaves them out completely. Kids spend eight hours a day learning things they may never use, while the skills that actually shape adulthood go untaught. Isn't that supposed to be the purpose of education? To prepare us for life?

But children don't spend their entire lives in school. So, the real question becomes:

What skills do we actually need to succeed in the real world?

Through my entrepreneurial struggles—the failures, the overwhelm, the small but meaningful victories—I was learning what no classroom ever taught me.

How to bounce back when things fall apart. How to solve problems in real time, without a rubric.
How to manage money, manage my mind, and stay grounded when everything felt uncertain. These weren't just business lessons; they were life lessons.

And I was learning them the hard way because no one had ever taught me that failure could be a teacher. That feeling overwhelmed could be a sign of growth. That small wins, stacked over time, could change everything.

Looking back, that's what education should have prepared me for: not just how to pass a test, but how to navigate the unknown. How to think for myself. How to keep going when there's no clear answer. That's what I finally learned one hard-earned lesson at a time.

For Entrepreneurial Parents: Business as Classroom

If you are building a business, you have a unique opportunity to provide your children with the real-world education that schools simply can't offer.

Having your kids work in your business isn't just about getting help; it's about giving them front-row seats to see how the adult world operates. They witness how you handle rejection when a sale doesn't go through. They observe how you problem-solve when technology fails or a customer complains. They see you adapt when a strategy that worked last month suddenly stops yielding results.

When I hired my teenagers to help with my Etsy shops, something beautiful happened. They weren't merely learning to upload listings or create mockups; they were developing resilience every time we had to pivot strategies. They learned emotional regulation by watching me manage stressful customer interactions. They gained financial literacy by seeing real money flowing in and out of business accounts.

Most importantly, they learned that failure is information. When a product didn't sell, we analyzed why together. When a marketing strategy flopped, we brainstormed alternatives. They received a real-time education in how successful adults navigate challenges.

Your business failures become their learning laboratories. Your customer service challenges turn into communication workshops. Your financial ups and downs transform into their economics classes, complete with real stakes and rewards.

The skills they were acquiring were adaptability, resilience, financial literacy, customer service, and problem-solving under pressure. These skills will be crucial for their success in adult life. And they are learning them in a safe environment where mistakes come with mentorship, not just consequences.

Creating Entrepreneurs Without a Business

But what if you don't have a business for your kids to work in? What if you are not an entrepreneur yourself but still want to impart these essential life skills?

The solution is to create entrepreneurial experiences within your home and community.

YouTube University with Payment Plans: There are countless valuable skills on YouTube that your kids could learn while earning money. Pay them to complete online courses in graphic design, video editing, coding, or digital marketing. Set milestones and payment schedules like a real job. When they struggle with a tutorial or their first attempt doesn't work, they learn that failure is part of the process, not a reason to quit.

Classic Kid Businesses That Teach Real Skills: The lemonade stand isn't outdated; it's entrepreneurship 101. Help your kids start small businesses: pet sitting, lawn care, tutoring younger kids, selling handmade crafts, or even a small online shop. Let them experience the full cycle: planning, investing their own money, marketing, dealing with difficult customers, and yes—failing sometimes.

Money Management in Real Time: Instead of theoretical math problems about compound interest, let them live it. Give them a budget for their business startup costs. Allow them to track expenses and profits. When their lemonade stand loses money due to overbuying supplies, that's a lesson no textbook can teach.

Creating Failure-Safe Environments: The key is to create environments where failure is safe yet real. Allow them to fail at small things now so they can handle bigger challenges later. When their pet-sitting business loses a client because they forgot to feed the fish, don't rescue them—help them problem-solve how to win the client back or avoid the mistake next time.

Don't protect your kids from failure; teach them to learn from it. Every setback they experience now, every rejection, every mistake, and every plan that falls apart builds the real-world skills that straight A's will never provide.

As I was growing through entrepreneurship, something unexpected began to shift at home, too. The way I handled challenges in business began to reshape how I parented. I stopped shielding myself and my kids from every mistake.

Instead of rushing to fix or avoid failure, I started making space for it. And in that space, something beautiful grew: confidence, creativity, and the quiet strength to keep going. Real growth, in business and in life, isn't about getting it right the first time. It's about having the courage to stay in the process long enough to become someone new.

CHAPTER 5

Design the Destination First

Building With Clarity in the Middle of the Climb

Before we dive into research, customer avatars, and product development, let's pause and talk about business for a moment— *real* business.

Business is different for everyone.

Some people start with an audience; others start with a dream. Some grow fast and messy; others grow slowly but strategically. For some, entrepreneurship is optional. For others, like the mom with kids depending on her, it's not.

And because it looks different for everyone, it will feel different, too. There will be moments that feel slow, discouraging, and confusing. There will be times when you put your heart into something and get silence in return. You will question if it's working. You will question if you *are* working.

That's not failure. That's **the valley**.

We all crave the mountaintop moment, the $10K month, the validation. But it doesn't show up at the start. It's waiting for you up ahead. And the only way to reach it is to keep walking, step by step, through the middle.

Progress is made through the mistakes, not around them. That's why you have to learn to get comfortable in the discomfort and keep walking with purpose.

Falling in the right direction, with buffers in place and lessons in motion. Because like we learned in Chapter 3, every failure is training your brain to become more efficient. You are not just stumbling; you are rewiring.

The truth is that tough skin is built by learning how to move through it with clarity. And clarity begins with knowing **who you are here to help**.

If you try to serve "everyone," you will dilute your efforts. If you build from assumption, you will waste energy on products no one's asking for. But when you root yourself in purpose and data, everything changes.

I learned that the hard way. At one point, I had five different Etsy shops, each with different products and target audiences. It felt like I was building five separate businesses at once—constantly shifting focus, constantly reacting. One day I was updating mockups for one shop, the next day I was rewriting listings for another. It was exhausting.

I thought splitting things up would make me more organized, more strategic. But it did the opposite. I couldn't test properly. I couldn't see what was working. I didn't know where to direct my energy, so I kept spreading it thin—and in the end, I felt unstable and overwhelmed.

That season taught me this: more isn't always better. Sometimes clarity comes from consolidating, not expanding. The sooner you define *who you are here to serve and how*, the sooner you can stop chasing stability and start building it.

When you build from this kind of clarity, everything shifts. We are not building just to stay busy. We are building to serve. To solve. To simplify.

We are going to walk through how to find your ideal customer, not with guesswork, but with evidence. You'll learn how to stop creating blindly and start building intentionally. Because every time you align your product with a real person's problem, you shorten the valley. You move a little closer to the top.

Let's build with people in mind, and let's build forward.

Success Looks Different for Everyone

This isn't a fixed number. It isn't a formula or a checklist of milestones you must reach by age 30 or 50. Success is personal. It evolves. And it's shaped by what you value in your current stage of life, whether that's freedom, stability, creativity, or growth.

In my early 20s, as a stay-at-home mom, I dreamed of making just $1,500 a month. I didn't hit that goal back then, mostly because fear and failure kept getting in the way. But if I could have made that amount, it would have changed everything.

That level of income would have given me choices. It would have allowed me to contribute financially without sacrificing time with my kids. At that point in my life, success wasn't about building an empire; it was about finding a way to support my family while still being fully present for them.

But today, success looks different. It's not just about paying bills or making a certain amount—it's about impact, freedom, and building a business that blesses my life and others. It's about creating with purpose and leaving a legacy.

And your definition of success will change too. As you grow—personally, spiritually, and professionally your goals will shift. What feels like a stretch today might feel like your baseline a year from now. Each win builds confidence. Each challenge builds courage. And that combination? It expands your vision.

You don't have to figure out your entire five-year plan today. But you do have to start. Because once you master one area and prove to yourself that you are capable, it unlocks something new in you. You stop asking, "Can I do this?" and start asking, "What else is possible?"

Don't compare your climb to someone else's mountaintop. Don't let social media trick you into thinking success is only found in six figures or luxury lifestyles.

Success might be:

- Finally launching that product you've been sitting on for six months.
- Making your first sale to someone who isn't a friend or family member.
- Creating a system that gives you back two hours of your day.
- Helping someone solve a problem you used to struggle with.

Honor your current version of success. Let it be enough for now, knowing that it's not the final destination. You are allowed to evolve. Your business is allowed to grow with you.

This journey isn't about rushing to a number; it's about becoming the kind of person who can build, sustain, and enjoy what they've created.

Define the Business You Are Building (Before You Build It)

You don't need a full business plan right now. But you do need direction. Clarity starts with understanding how you want your business to operate today. Not six months from now, not in theory, but in real life with your current time, energy, and goals.

Ask yourself:

What kind of business are you actually trying to build right now—and who is it for?

Your answer matters. Not just for planning, but for protecting your focus.

Because until you know who you are serving and how you want to serve them, everything else will feel scattered.

Some people start with one core product. Others launch with a storefront full of offers. Some begin with services and layer in digital products later. There's no wrong path, but you need to choose a starting point that fits your vision and your capacity.

The Core Product Approach

This model is focused. You create one offer—maybe a course, a guide, a template, or a service—and you become known for it.

When done well, this approach builds authority fast because your energy isn't scattered. You are focused on one solution, one audience, one message. That kind of focus creates clarity, and clarity creates results.

And because you are not juggling ten things at once, you can scale faster. Your attention isn't scattered, and you are not experimenting in five different directions. You are building depth in one, and that's what creates real momentum.

If you are someone who thrives with structure and clarity, this model can create momentum fast. But it also requires discipline. You need to be okay saying no to every "extra" until that one product is solid.

The Storefront Model

This model is all about variety. You create multiple products: digital downloads, courses, resources, maybe bundles and organize them into a shop or marketplace.

Your customers may come in for different reasons. Some want a low-ticket product. Some want something more in-depth. This model allows you to serve more people at different entry points.

The challenge? It takes more upfront content creation. You'll need systems to keep everything organized. And because your attention is spread across products, it can take longer to optimize each one.

This model is ideal for creatives who love building, testing, and managing multiple assets at once.

The Skills-Based Model

This model is for hands-on entrepreneurs, the ones who create, teach, or serve through a practical skill. Maybe you bake, sew, braid, style, consult, or teach people how to manage money. You've got a skill, and now you want to turn it into income.

This model usually starts small and personal—one client, one order, one service at a time. But don't underestimate its potential. When you build with intention, you can grow from a side hustle into a scalable business.

The challenge? This model often starts with trading time for money. That's why structure matters. You need a business plan that protects your energy while growing your impact.

Over time, many skill-based entrepreneurs layer in digital elements—like recipes, patterns, guides, or how-to workshops—so they can earn passively, even when they're not working hands-on.

If you're someone with a valuable skill and a desire to build from that skillset, this model gives you a grounded place to start and grow.

The Hybrid Model

Maybe you already have a service-based business—a coaching practice, tax firm, or design agency—and now you want to add digital products.

You are not replacing your service. You are building a second stream of income that runs even when you are not in meetings or client work.

That could look like:

- Selling a digital version of something you teach often.
- Turning FAQs into a downloadable guide.

- Offering templates that support your client process.

This model gives you flexibility. It helps you create time leverage. But you still need a strategy because you'll be managing two business types: one hands-on and one automated.

Other Paths That Start with People

Not every business starts with a product. Some start with a platform. Others start with a gathering.

The next two models, Content Creator and Community-First take a different approach. They don't lead with a clear offer right away. Instead, they start by building trust, creating conversations, and serving consistently.

These models may take longer to monetize at first, but when done with purpose, they can lead to powerful, profitable businesses.

If you're someone who thrives on connection, storytelling, or showing up online, these might be the seeds of your success.

The Content Creator Model

Some people don't start with a product; they start with a platform. They create content. They post videos. They build an audience. And then one day... that audience wants more.

This model begins with attention. You're not selling something right away; you're building visibility, trust, and momentum. You become known for your content, and later, you monetize that influence.

That might look like:

- Affiliate marketing for products you believe in

- Creating a digital product that solves the exact problem your audience keeps asking about
- Launching a subscription or paid community
- Partnering with brands through sponsorships

The challenge? It can be slow to start, especially if you don't already have an audience. You're investing time in consistent content creation, often before you earn your first dollar.

But once you understand what your audience needs and how you can help, engagement turns into income. Because where there's attention, there's opportunity.

This model is ideal for people who enjoy creating, teaching, or sharing online. If you have a message, a niche, or even just a curiosity you want to explore publicly, this can be a powerful way to build.

Just remember: even if your business starts with content, it still needs direction. Go viral with purpose, not confusion. Let the problems your audience is facing guide what you offer next.

The Community-First Model

This model starts with connection. Before you ever create a product, you gather people around a shared need, identity, or goal. You build trust. You lead conversations. You create a space where people feel seen.

Sometimes it's a Facebook group. Sometimes it's a local meetup. Sometimes it's a movement that lives online. And eventually, you realize: this community needs something more. That's when the business begins.

That might look like:

- Launching a digital product that solves a shared struggle
- Turning the group into a paid membership
- Hosting live workshops, masterminds, or retreats

The key to this model is listening. The best community leaders don't assume; they ask. They stay close to the needs of the people they're serving, and when the time is right, they offer something deeper.

This model can overlap with the Hybrid or Storefront approach, but what makes it unique is this: the relationships come first.

If you're someone who naturally builds community, don't underestimate that gift. With care and intention, it can become the foundation of a powerful and lasting business.

Model	How It Starts	Best For	Primary Focus	Monetization Timing
Core Product	One focused offer (course, template, service, etc.)	Creators who want clarity and structure	Solving one big problem	Medium
Storefront	Multiple offers in a shop or marketplace	Builders who like variety and flexibility	Offering multiple solutions	Medium–Fast
Skills-Based	Hands-on service using a skill (braiding, coaching, etc.)	Entrepreneurs with a teachable skill	Turning skill into income	Medium–Fast
Hybrid	Existing service + added digital products	Service pros wanting passive income	Leveraging time with scalable tools	Medium
Explorer	No clear idea yet—starts by researching problems	Beginners with curiosity	Learning by doing + problem discovery	Medium–Slow

Content Creator	Building an audience through value-driven content	Creators who enjoy teaching or sharing	Attention, trust, then monetization	Slow (then exponential)
Community-First	Gathering people around a shared goal or need	Natural connectors, community builders	Leading, then offering support	Slow–Medium

Decide Where to Begin

You don't need to have everything figured out before you start. But you do need to move.

Business clarity doesn't come from sitting on ideas. It comes from taking action—imperfectly, but intentionally. The best time to start isn't when things feel perfect. It's right now.

Ask yourself:

- Do I want to be known for one product and go deep?
- Do I want to offer a variety of solutions and build a storefront?
- Do I have a skill I can turn into income?
- Do I want to build a platform by sharing content and building trust?
- Do I already lead a community that's ready for more?

Still unsure? Start here: What's the problem you want to solve?

Every business model in this book works—but only if it's built around a real need. You don't need a blueprint. You need a problem worth solving and the courage to start solving it.

Your business will evolve. What you start with may not be what you're known for a year from now. That's normal. You're playing the long game. You're building something sustainable, not chasing a quick fix. So don't delay. Start small. Start focused. But whatever you do—start.

You've chosen a path—or at least you're moving in the direction of one. Now it's time to build. But how do you make sure what you're building actually matters to the people you want to serve?

That's where strategy comes in. Not hustle. Not guesswork. Just a clear, proven approach that helps you build the right product, for the right person, at the right time.

The Key to Progress: Backwards Design

Before we dive into building your first (or next) offer, I want to introduce you to a strategy that can completely shift the way you approach product creation.

It's called **backwards design**, and it's how you stop wasting time creating things people don't actually want and start building with purpose.

This method isn't new. In fact, it's borrowed from the world of education, where teachers use it to plan their lessons by starting with the desired outcome and then working backward. What do we want the student to know or be able to do? And what steps will help them get there?

In business, it works the same way. Instead of starting with, *"What should I sell?"* we ask, *"What transformation do I want to help someone achieve?"* And then we reverse-engineer a path to that result.

This strategy only works if you are approaching your business with the right mindset. If you are rushing to create just to make money, backwards design will feel like a slowdown. But if you understand that clarity leads to confidence, and confidence leads to consistency, then this approach will save you hours, dollars, and disappointment.

We will break down exactly how to use backwards design later in this chapter. But I'm planting the seed now because once you learn to think like this, it will change how you build, how you sell, and how you succeed.

The Business Is What You Build— But You're Who You Become

Remember: you don't eat an elephant in one bite. You don't build a successful business overnight. But with one sale, one solved problem, one clear lesson at a time. That's how you become the entrepreneur you are meant to be. But here's the biggest truth of all:

The process shapes the person. You don't just hit an income goal—you become someone who can *sustain* it.

The learning, the trial and error, the consistency despite the discouragement—that's the work that transforms you. And that's why your why has to be bigger than your dollar goal. Because when the money doesn't show up as fast as you hoped (and sometimes it won't), you need something deeper to anchor you.

If your only reason for building this business is to hit a number, you will start over every time that number feels out of reach. But if you are building something rooted in purpose, something that reminds you of your long-term vision, you will keep going even on the days when nothing sells.

Write your why down. Post it somewhere visible. Return to it every time you start to doubt.

And when the discouragement creeps in, repeat one of these affirmations out loud until your mindset realigns:

Business Affirmations for When You Feel Like Quitting

- I am building something that will bless my life and others— one step at a time.
- I don't have to be perfect—I just have to be consistent.
- Every challenge is shaping me into the business owner I'm becoming.
- My progress may be quiet, but it is still progress.
- I trust the process, even when the results aren't instant.
- I don't chase success. I attract it by showing up and serving.
- There is room for me in this market. No one can duplicate my vision.
- I am building something valuable brick by brick, day by day.
- I trust GOD with the results; I focus on faith and obedience.

Now breathe. Re-center. Pick one thing and do it today. That's how you build a business that lasts. And once your mindset is realigned, you are ready for the next step: starting, even if it's imperfect.

Why Small Wins Build Big Belief

You don't need a five-figure launch to prove you are a real business owner. You need proof that you are moving. That you are building. That someone, somewhere, received value from something you made, and it mattered.

That's why I teach people to chase small wins first. Because momentum breeds belief. And belief is what keeps you going when the sales are slow, the algorithm is silent, and imposter syndrome starts shouting louder than your goals.

Getting your product into the market faster means receiving feedback sooner, and that feedback is the fastest way to grow. Every time you hit publish, you learn. Every time someone buys, even just one person, you get real-time proof that you are solving a problem, not just dreaming about one.

You are not just pretending to be in business; you are in business. You made something from nothing. You served someone. You took your idea and released it into the world. That's not small. That's bold.

But here's where many new entrepreneurs get stuck:
They start with big financial goals—$5K/month, $10K/month, replace a full-time income. And while those goals are valid, they shouldn't be the only reason you are building a business.

Why?

Because when the income doesn't show up right away (and it rarely does), it can feel like failure. That disappointment hits differently. It doesn't just affect your strategy; it affects your belief. And belief is what carries you through the valley.

Still, confidence is only part of the story. What really anchors you is becoming the kind of person who can thrive even when the income is delayed. You should focus on confidence wins before income wins.

We all want to make money; I get it. But money alone won't anchor you. What does? A clear path, belief in your vision, and the discipline to show up—even when sales are slow and doubts get loud. And that confidence? It's built by stacking small wins, one after another, until the big wins have no choice but to follow.

Here's what a small win might look like:

- You published your first product even if no one bought it yet.
- You created a freebie, and three people signed up for your email list.
- You made your first $7 sale.
- Someone shared your post because it helped them.
- You got a message saying, "Thank you, I needed this."
- You opened your Etsy shop or set up your Shopify store.
- You showed up consistently this week, even when you didn't feel confident.
- You made progress without needing perfection.

These aren't just tasks. They are declarations:
"I'm here."
"I'm building."
"I'm not giving up."

Celebrate every single one. Because these wins are the bricks that build belief. And belief is what creates the kind of consistency that outlasts every setback.

Start With the Problem, Not the Product

Before you even think about strategy or revenue, you need to ask a more important question:

Who am I helping, and what problem am I solving?

If you are building a product without solving a real need, you are skipping the foundation, and no marketing strategy can fix that later. Too many people start by asking, *"What can I sell?"* But the real question is: *"What do they need?"*

Because profit doesn't come from pretty products. It comes from real solutions. You are not here to build a cluttered digital storefront.

You are here to build **solutions.** To use your ideas, your skills, your voice to meet someone in their struggle and help them move forward. That's what makes this work worth doing.

And once you are clear on the problem, you can build the solution from scratch. Not randomly. Not reactively. But intentionally, with focus, purpose, and impact.

Ask yourself:

- Who is my ideal customer?
- What are they struggling with right now?
- What's keeping them stuck, frustrated, or overwhelmed?
- Is my product a "nice to **have**" or a "need to **have**"?
- What transformation am I promising?

Because when you focus on solving a real problem for a real person, your entire business gets lighter. You stop overthinking. You stop chasing every shiny idea. And you start building like someone who knows why they're here.

Backwards Design: Planning a Business That Starts With the End in Mind

Here's how I approach the next step, using a strategy pulled from my years in education called backwards design. It's a planning method where you start with the end result in mind and then work backward to figure out the steps to get there.

In teaching, it looked like this:

- First, define the learning outcome.
- Then, plan the lesson around achieving that outcome.

In business, it works the same way but with one powerful shift:

You don't start by asking, "What should I sell?" You start by asking:

"What transformation do I want to help someone experience?"

Let's See This in Action: Idea Discovery

No matter how good your ideas sound in your head, it's the data that makes them worth building.

This is where most entrepreneurs get stuck, not because they lack creativity, but because they don't know where to start. Some people come in with a niche in mind but aren't sure what to create. Others have no clue what they want to sell; they just know they want to build something meaningful.

Either way, clarity starts with research. You don't need fancy tools or expensive software. You just need the willingness to look, listen, and observe what real people are struggling with. That's where the best products are born—in response to real-world needs.

Below, I'll show you two different paths. Both start with research, but each is designed for a different type of starting point.

Option 1: You Have No Idea What to Sell Yet

You are starting with a blank slate, but you still need a general direction. Don't worry; you don't need a perfect idea to get started. Just curiosity and a willingness to listen. Here's how to begin.

Start by reflecting on where your interests, experiences, or curiosity naturally lead you. Think about:

- The YouTube videos you've watched recently.
- The Facebook groups you are already a part of.
- The blog posts or forums you tend to explore.
- Conversations that keep catching your attention.

These breadcrumbs matter. Once you have identified a general interest area—parenting, wellness, productivity, side hustles—go research. Use tools like:

- **AnswerThePublic**—see what people are asking about that topic.
- **Reddit**—read real frustrations and solutions being shared in niche communities.
- **YouTube comments**—what questions are viewers asking under niche-specific videos?

- **Pinterest**—search problems, not products (e.g., "how to stay organized as a new mom").

At this stage, your job is not to create; it's to observe. Gather clues, spot patterns, and start writing down the problems you see repeated over and over. You don't need to have a solution yet. Just get obsessed with understanding what people are actually struggling with.

Then ask yourself:
→ Is this a problem I can solve?
→ Can I create something simple that would genuinely help them take one step forward?

Option 2: You Have a Niche in Mind, But Need to Validate the Idea

Maybe you already have a group of people you want to help, but you are not sure what to offer. Let me show you how I've worked through this myself.

Let's say I want to create a product for moms who feel overwhelmed during the school year. At first glance, that sounds like a niche. But instead of guessing what they need, I go straight to the data.

Yes, I've lived that chaos. I've forgotten picture day. I've missed deadlines for field trip money. I've had to double back home because someone forgot their folder again. But personal experience can only guide the idea—it can't validate it. And most importantly, I am not creating a product just for me.

I begin validating the idea. I visit Facebook groups filled with moms juggling school schedules. I scroll through Reddit parenting threads, mom blogs, and YouTube comment sections. Quickly, I start seeing a pattern. Moms are asking:

- "How do you keep up with all the school events?"
- "Anyone have a system for after-school routines that actually works?"
- "What helps you stay organized when everything hits at once—sports, homework, dinner?"

That's my green light. This isn't just a one-off complaint. It's a documented, recurring struggle.

To confirm the demand, I plug key phrases into tools like:

- **AnswerThePublic** – to see what real moms are searching for
- **Pinterest** – to explore trends, tips, and content engagement
- **Google autocomplete** – to discover what questions people are typing in first

Now that I've confirmed the demand, I define the transformation I want to offer:

I want to help busy moms go from feeling overwhelmed and reactive to feeling calm, prepared, and confident throughout the school year. With that outcome in mind, I can build the right product—not just a cute download, but a meaningful solution.

Because once you define the transformation, you are not just selling a file. You are delivering relief, progress, and hope to someone who needs it most.

From Data to Impact

Before you move on, double-check your idea:

- Does your customer walk away with a skill, feeling, or result?
- Can you describe the outcome in one sentence?
- Would your product still be valuable even if they didn't know your name?

Be careful not to confuse features with transformation.

"25-page journal" is a feature.
"Helps moms create a 5-minute morning routine that reduces stress before school drop-off" is a transformation.

Once your transformation is clear, then you are ready to plan your product using backwards design.

Applying Backwards Design:

Now that you have identified a clear transformation, it's time to reverse-engineer your product. This is where backwards design turns an idea into a solution.

Instead of starting with, "What can I make?" you start with,
"What does my customer need to experience, believe, or do by the end?"

Then, you work backwards:

1. **Break the transformation into smaller outcomes.** What milestones or steps will help your customer get from stuck to success?
2. **Design content or tools that support each step.** Whether it's a guide, planner, template, or worksheet—ask yourself: "Will this actually move them closer to the result?"

3. **Organize your product around those outcomes.** Make the layout clear, logical, and purposeful. Every page should serve a specific part of the transformation.

Real Example:

Let's go back to the earlier idea:

Transformation: Help overwhelmed moms feel more organized and in control during the school year.

Here's how you might work backwards from that:

Mini Outcomes:

- Stop missing important school events
- Create smoother after-school transitions
- Feel more calm and prepared each morning

Product Components:

- A printable weekly calendar with space for school events, meals, and notes
- A morning checklist that kids can follow independently
- A visual after-school routine chart with step-by-step structure

Each piece isn't just "cute" or "aesthetic." It's there for a reason. It solves something. It leads somewhere.

Final Check:

When you are done, ask yourself:

- Is this product actionable?
- Is it simple to implement?
- Will it give someone a small but meaningful win?

That's what backwards design does. It grounds creativity in strategy. It turns scattered ideas into clear, helpful offers that people *actually* want to buy.

Start with Data, Not Assumptions Checklist

Use this step-by-step guide to discover real problems and design real solutions:

Step 1: Identify your general niche or audience
Who do you want to help (e.g., moms, small business owners, teachers)?
What stage are they in (just starting, overwhelmed, scaling)?

Step 2: Go research the real-world problems
Search Facebook groups, Reddit, YouTube comments
Look at Pinterest, Google, or AnswerThePublic for common questions and complaints
Write down the most frequent problems, frustrations, or obstacles they mention

Step 3: Define the transformation
What outcome are they craving?
How can you help them move from point A (stuck) to point B (solution)?
Is the product solving a need to have or just a nice to have problem?

Step 4: Reverse-engineer the product
What small, focused product would support that outcome?
Can it be delivered as a digital download, template, guide, or planner?

Does it make their life easier or more successful in a measurable way?

Step 5: Build and test

Create a beta version

Put it in front of a small audience

Gather feedback and refine before scaling

When You Don't Feel Like an Expert Yet

Let's pause here because this might be the moment your inner critic starts whispering:

"But who am I to teach this?"

"I'm not an expert."

"There are people way more qualified than me."

You are not alone in that feeling. Almost every creator hits that wall. But here's what I want you to remember: **expertise isn't something you wait to feel; it's something you build by doing.**

If you have helped one or two people solve a problem—even if one of them was yourself—you are already further along than someone else. That's the foundation of service. That's where credibility begins.

Think about the areas of life where you are naturally good at something. Maybe it's organizing chaos, writing with clarity, explaining complicated topics simply, or finding creative ways to motivate kids. You might not have a certification in it, but you've lived it. You've figured something out. And someone out there needs that exact insight.

The truth is no one starts as an expert. The only way to become one is to show up consistently, keep learning, and stay committed to helping. The more you do it, the clearer your voice becomes. The more you build, the better your solutions get. That's how real expertise is formed: not from perfection, but from progress.

There's a saying that *"practice makes perfect,"* but here's the truth: practice doesn't make you perfect. Practice makes you better. And better is the goal.

So, release the pressure to have it all figured out. Start with what you know. Build with what you learn. Deliver with heart. Because done imperfectly, with real care, is always better than perfect in your head.

You are ready. Not because you have all the answers, but because you are willing to show up, solve a problem, and grow in the process. And that? That's the mark of a true entrepreneur.

Build with Intention

Clarity doesn't come from having all the answers; it comes from asking better questions and being brave enough to begin. In this chapter, you have learned how to use backwards design to build with purpose, not pressure. Whether you are starting with a blank slate or refining an idea, your path forward isn't built on perfection; it's built on action.

You don't need to be an expert to start. You don't need to get it all right. You just need to care enough to solve a real problem—and take the next step. This is your permission to begin with what you have, trust what you are learning, and build as you go. The clarity will come. The confidence will grow. But only if you start.

Still stuck on what to create?

If you are ready to get started but feel overwhelmed by the blank page, don't worry, there's another option. You can begin by customizing done-for-you digital products and templates designed to help you build quickly without sacrificing quality.

I created ElevateHerVault.com for women just like you—entrepreneurs who are ready to move from idea to action, even if they're still figuring things out. Every product in the shop is crafted with clarity, confidence, and growth in mind.

Head to the vault and find something you can start with *today*.

Chapter 6
How to Build Your Failure Portfolio

Why My Worst Business Moments Made Me a Better Entrepreneur

I'll show you how to turn every failed launch, missed goal, and messy lesson into fuel for your next breakthrough, starting with the same simple tool that changed everything for me: a Failure Portfolio.

I used to treat my business failures like dirty laundry—hiding them deep in the back of my mental closet, hoping no one would notice the smell of disappointment or the cost of wasted time. But here's what I learned: when you bury your failures, they don't disappear. They quietly start to define you. Instead of learning from them, you start working around them. And the more you hide, the heavier it gets.

It was the slow, quiet buildup—the frustration every time I hesitated to launch, the exhaustion from chasing perfect timing, the guilt of half-finished ideas collecting dust. I was trapped in a cycle of starting, stopping, and second-guessing, unsure how to break free.

Late one night, I had a hard conversation with myself, the kind you can't sugarcoat.

I sat there, exhausted and frustrated, and said out loud: *"You have a master's in education. You are a teacher. Your whole life has been about solving problems and helping people grow. So, why aren't you treating your business the same way?"*

That moment snapped me into a different mode. I stopped thinking like a dreamer and started thinking like a problem-solver. I decided to look at my failures like data, as a teacher would approach a struggling student. What's working? What's not? What patterns keep repeating? What small, sustainable changes can I try?

Because at the rate I was going, nothing was changing. And I knew: if I wanted a different result, I had to change the way I responded to failure.

I grabbed a pen and started writing. Not a plan for the future, but a breakdown of the past. Raw, unfiltered thoughts about what felt heavy, what kept going wrong, and what I was scared to admit.

One of the first things I wrote was this:

"Course Success That Became a Burden: Made $1,000 on hiring kids' course with minimal promotion. Should feel like a win. Instead, I feel paralyzed by tax updates and perfectionism. Taking it down rather than fixing it. This pattern of self-sabotage has to stop."

That single reflection was a turning point. I realized I didn't need to go bigger. I needed to go simpler.

No more massive projects that left me drained every time something needed updating. No more putting all my energy into one complicated launch. I needed an approach that felt sustainable, not suffocating.

So, I made a shift: smaller offers, simpler products, and faster feedback. *That was all my faith muscle could hold at the time—and that was enough. I wasn't giving up; I was giving myself something I could actually carry until I got stronger.*

And it started with that notebook. Over time, those scribbled thoughts became what I now call my **Failure Portfolio**—a living document of insights, patterns, and lessons that changed how I built my business.

I'll show you how to create your own. Because once you stop seeing failure as something to avoid and start seeing it as your most powerful teacher, you finally start building the business you are meant to lead.

From Shame Spiral to Success Strategy

Here's what nobody tells you about successful entrepreneurs: we fail constantly. The difference is, we fail knowing that those mistakes are helping us grow. We collect our failures like some people collect stamps—methodically, purposefully, and with the understanding that each one adds value to our collection.

Success isn't just about the launch. It's about learning to lead, sustain, and evolve with the business you are building. The early stages aren't just about strategy or sales; they're about resilience, honesty, and growth. Each misstep is data. Every setback is a mirror. Our businesses don't just grow because of strategy—they grow because we do.

Failure isn't just part of the process; it *is* the training ground. My failure journal isn't pretty. It's actually two notebooks. I lost the first one during a particularly overwhelming period and started a second, then found the original one later. That's how scattered I was in the early days.

Both notebooks are filled with honest confessions, dollar amounts that make me cringe, and lessons that hurt to learn. But they're also the documents I refer to most when making business decisions.

I didn't know it at the time, but this format became my personal business lab—each entry a mini case study. Every entry follows the same brutally honest framework:

- What I tried (usually with excessive confidence)
- How much it cost me (time, money, sanity)
- Why it failed (the real reason, not the excuse I told myself)
- What I learned (the lesson worth the tuition)
- How I'll use this knowledge (the practical application)

The magic happens when you start seeing patterns. I often underestimate timelines and consistently overestimate demand for things I'm personally excited about. I have a weakness for shiny new tools that promise to solve all my problems.

Try writing just one of these entries this week. You'll be surprised how much clarity you gain—not just about your business, but about yourself.

Case Study: The $15,000+ Program That Nearly Broke Me

Let me pull back the curtain on the biggest "failure" that almost broke me—and ultimately saved me. At the time, I was drowning in confusion. I had already invested in several coaches, watched every free training I could find, and tried to follow a dozen strategies to grow my first shop. But nothing was working. I felt stuck, exhausted, and on the edge of giving up.

So, when I saw the $15,000 business program, it felt like a lifeline. *Finally*, I thought. *This is it. This is how I'm going to make it.* I didn't hesitate. I clicked "buy now," convinced that this was the breakthrough I'd been praying for.

But once I logged into the member portal and saw the massive list of modules, my excitement quickly turned into overwhelm. It wasn't the program's fault—it was my mindset. Even with access to coaches and resources, I felt paralyzed. I couldn't see a clear path forward because I was mentally stuck. And when you feel stuck, even good advice can feel like pressure.

Looking back, I realized the program was full of valuable guidance. But at the time, I was trying to do everything all at once—create content, post daily, launch new products, manage multiple shops, and show up on every platform. I wasn't focused. I wasn't grounded. I was chasing results instead of building a foundation.

What overwhelm actually looked like in my life:

I stopped thinking clearly. I was jumping from shop to shop like a pinball—frantically trying to figure out what to create next, where to post, and which business needed my attention most. The shop I was "supposed" to focus on was barely making $100–$120 a month, but I was expected to give it my full attention while my other businesses quietly withered.

Sleep became a luxury. I'd lie awake at 3 AM thinking about content calendars, Instagram posts, and product creation. I'd squeeze in an hour of work before my day job, then collapse back at my computer at night—working until I literally fell asleep at my desk.

Food? Whatever was fastest. Movement? Nonexistent. As my clothes got tighter, I ignored every signal my body was screaming at me.

And when I reached out to the coaching support, hoping for clarity, the answers often left me more confused than before. Not because they weren't helpful, but because my mind wasn't clear enough to receive them. I was still clinging to other shops, scared to let go of what was familiar, even if it wasn't sustainable. How could I abandon something that made *some* money to give my all to something that wasn't even covering groceries?

But the real breaking point wasn't business; it was personal. I started snapping at the people I loved most, all because of my own insecurity. The truth is, how you view yourself in business often mirrors how you view yourself in life. The less confident I felt in my business, the worse I felt about myself as a person.

I set impossible income goals based on projections, then beat myself up when I didn't hit them. I'd tell myself, *"I can't work full-time, complete this program, AND manage multiple shops."* So, I'd pause the program—then crawl back weeks later, guilty over how much I had invested.

I was working so hard, but not smart. And when you're not thinking clearly, you can't move forward. You just stay stuck. They told me to hire a VA to help manage everything. It did help—kind of. But now I had to train someone in a system I barely understood myself. It felt like starting all over again.

That's when I realized: I had to choose. Follow their system—or take my life back. Not because the program didn't work. But because *I* couldn't work the program—not in the mental and emotional state I was in.

Sometimes it's not the program that needs to change—it's the season we're in, or the pace we're trying to run at. I wasn't broken. I was just burnt out. Once I slowed down, got clear, and gave myself permission to focus, everything started to shift.

Lessons from Building My Portfolio

I didn't truly begin to understand what was working in my business—or what wasn't—until I started journaling. That's when I realized I had been tracking my progress by the wrong markers. I measured success only by numbers. If I didn't hit a specific income goal, I thought I had failed.

But journaling helped me zoom out. I began to see patterns—habits that drained me, mindsets that kept me stuck, and quiet wins I had completely overlooked. The more I wrote, the more I realized I was building something meaningful. I wasn't just creating products—I was becoming someone new. And that, more than any strategy, changed everything.

Here are a few lessons I uncovered while reflecting on my portfolio journey:

The Perfectionist Product Prison (8 months of delay)

I spent months "almost ready," constantly tweaking, improving, and perfecting—while others were selling imperfect products that actually helped people. I learned that perfect products don't make an impact. *Published* ones do.

The Underpricing Trap (thousands in missed income)

I priced my services like I was apologizing for existing. That only attracted clients who expected everything for nothing—and resented me when they didn't get it. I worked twice as hard for half the money. Eventually, I learned that charging what I'm worth isn't arrogance—it's alignment.

The Social Media Black Hole

I posted where I thought I *should* be instead of where my actual audience was. Once I paid attention to who was engaging—and where—I stopped wasting time and started building connections.

But the biggest shift?

I stopped chasing strategy and started developing self-trust. Instead of clinging to old wins or future goals, I got honest about what I needed *right now*. I stopped trying to become a different person and started becoming more of myself—focused, grounded, and clear.

Because **the becoming is always more important than the outcome**. And once you commit to the becoming, the outcome eventually has no choice but to follow.

That's why I created my own "Failure Portfolio"—a space to reflect honestly on what didn't work and how I turned those lessons into growth. And now, I want you to start one, too.

Small Experiments, Big Shifts

You've seen how failure shaped my story, but this isn't just about me. It's about you. The only way to truly grow from failure is to get honest about it. Not just once, but often. That's why I created my own "Failure Portfolio," and I want you to start one, too.

Think of this as your first step into the work. We'll revisit this tool later, but you don't need the full blueprint to begin. Sometimes clarity comes after action. Start here—while the insight is still sharp.

Open a document or grab a notebook. Title it: My Failure Portfolio. Write your first entry today and mark the date.

Pick one "failure" from your past—something that didn't go as planned but taught you something valuable. Don't overthink it. Just take 5-10 minutes and jot down whatever comes to mind. Use this simple format if it helps:

- What happened?
- What did you learn?
- How do you use that lesson now?

Take a deep breath—this is the work. Naming your failures with honesty and curiosity is where real transformation begins.

This is just a practice run. We'll dive deeper into the full method later, but for now, let your thoughts flow.

Congratulations! You just turned your mistakes into momentum.

The Experiment That Changed My Bank Account

After cataloging my failures, I began to approach business differently. Instead of making huge, life-altering decisions, I started running small experiments.

Want to test a new service? Don't build a whole website; just send an email to ten past clients. Curious about a new market? Don't pivot your entire business; create one piece of content and see who responds. Thinking about raising prices? Don't rebrand everything; test with the next three proposals. (I tried this in one of my shops, and it didn't increase the value as I had hoped.)

This shift from "all or nothing" to "let's see what happens" made failure feel less daunting and success more attainable. Instead of betting the farm, I was betting lunch money.

My Current Experiment Practice: My goal now, based on my data, is to focus on my own content creation—whether that's a book I'll publish, a course I'm developing, or digital products I'll create for other business owners to resell. I'm only spending money on things that directly support this mission.

What I'm about to share is just one snapshot from my current experiment. It may evolve by the time you read this, but the insight still holds true.

One recent experiment was launching a brand-new Instagram account for one of my digital product businesses. In just one month, I grew it from zero to over 600 followers—which felt exciting at first. But when I looked closer, only two people actually joined my mailing list.

That single test taught me something important: growth doesn't always mean progress. And just because something looks like it's working on the surface doesn't mean it's aligned with my goal.

Through this process, I realized Instagram might not be the platform where I want to build long-term—and that's okay. That's the point of testing: to figure out where your energy actually belongs.

When you are first starting out, you are doing it all—creating the product, building the site, managing the social media, answering the emails. Trying to build on multiple platforms at the same time doesn't make you more successful; it makes you more exhausted. That's why the smartest thing you can do is pick one platform, master it, and then expand once you've got systems or support in place.

Instead of spreading myself thin, I'm choosing to test and focus. And based on everything I've learned from this experiment, I've decided to lean into YouTube. The content lasts longer, it fits how I teach, and it gives me the space to show up in a way that feels aligned and sustainable.

That clarity came from testing, not guessing, and it reminded me that experiments aren't failures; they're filters. The key is treating every test as data collection, not as a verdict on my potential. Whether an experiment succeeds or fails, it's moving me closer to understanding what works for my business and my life.

The Hidden ROI of Getting It Wrong

Every mistake I made taught me something more valuable than money. It taught me how I work best. I used to chase every program and stretch myself across too many businesses. Now I create with clarity, based on how I actually function, not how someone else says I should.

Turns out, that $15K failure wasn't a waste. It was tuition. And it taught me to stop tolerating what doesn't work.

Creating Your Own Safe Space to Fail

The goal isn't to avoid failure; it's to fail *smart*. Here's how I create safe spaces to experiment without risking everything:

- **The $100 Rule** – I never spend more than $100 testing an idea until I see results.
- **The Two-Week Test** – I give new ideas two weeks max to show promise.
- **The Emotion Check** – If I'm getting overly attached to an outcome, I pause. Curiosity over ego.
- **The Support System** – I surround myself with people who understand that failure is just research in disguise.

This simple framework helps me take bold action without burning out. I get to dream big while risking small. Because here's the truth: There are no failed experiments—only successful market research. Now that you know how to think about failure, let's talk about how to organize it.

Your Failure Portfolio: The Fulfill Framework

You see that it takes real work to actually look at yourself and get to the reasons why we make the choices we do. I joined a program to help fix a problem, but I realized I was the problem. I knew it was my mindset, but I didn't know how deep those roots went.

Our school system's pass/fail behavior follows us into adulthood, but we cannot approach entrepreneurship this way. In school, if I worked really hard, I'd get better grades, teacher approval, and advancement to the next level. But entrepreneurship doesn't work like that. In entrepreneurship, you work hard AND smart, but it may take time to see the progress you are looking for.

Think about bamboo. It grows underground for five years, and no one sees it working. You could walk on top of it and not notice anything happening. But after those five years, the elevation happens—it can grow up to 90 feet in just six weeks. We have to trust this same process in business.

The failure portfolio isn't just about documenting what went wrong. It's about excavating the deeper patterns, the unconscious beliefs, and the inherited behaviors that keep us stuck. Sometimes the most expensive programs teach us the most valuable lessons—not about business strategy, but about ourselves.

Two Formats to Fit Your Life

The key to extracting value from your failures isn't just remembering what happened; it's asking the right questions to uncover the lessons hiding in the experience. There are two ways to use this tool, and you can choose whichever fits your time and mindset:

- **The Simple Format** – quick bullet points or short answers to document a lesson fast.
- **The Detailed Format** – a deeper dive that helps you unpack patterns, emotions, and long-term takeaways.

I've developed two formats depending on how much time you have and how complex the situation was:

The Simple Format (5-10 minutes)

Perfect for quick lessons and building the habit:

What happened? A brief, honest summary of the situation without drama or judgment.

What did you learn? The main insight or lesson from this experience.

How do you use that lesson now? How has this learning influenced your decisions or approach since then?

The Detailed Format (15-20 minutes)

For bigger setbacks or when you want deeper insights:

What did you try? Be specific about what you attempted. What truly happened? Remove all biases.

What did it cost you? (time, money, energy) Include all the real costs. Time spent creating, money invested in tools or ads, and emotional energy drained by the process. This helps you understand the true investment and ROI of the learning.

Why didn't it work? This is where you dig past the surface. Not "people didn't buy it" but "people didn't buy it because I was solving a problem they complained about but wouldn't pay to fix," or "I was targeting the right people with the wrong message."

What did you learn from it? Focus on insights you can apply elsewhere. What did this teach you about your market, your messaging, your assumptions, or your process?

How will you use this lesson going forward? Make it actionable. What will you do differently next time? What will you test? What will you avoid?

Pro Tip: Always include the date of both the failure and when you are writing about it. You'll be amazed at how your perspective on the same experience changes over time, and those shifts in perspective are valuable data too.

Now that you've seen how the Detailed Format works, here's an example straight from my own Failure Portfolio. This reflection came after one of the most expensive learning experiences I've had in business.

Real Portfolio Example:
The $15,000+ Program (Detailed Format)

Let me show you exactly how this works with my own biggest "failure":

Date of failure: July 2024

Date of reflection: May 20, 2025

What did I try? I only implemented some of the things. I watched the modules, but I made excuses that I didn't like the flow. The coaches told me to let my other shops go, but they were my money makers, so I worked in all the shops instead, which created more confusion. I hired a VA in 2025 to help with things in my other shops (no help in 2024 because I took so many pauses from the coaching program). Then I hired a different VA to manage Pinterest to Facebook for a month. When I watched live trainings, I would focus on the worst-case scenarios, like "your listing images should look like this," then I'd immediately hire someone to fix them. I'd ask my coach about it after I'd already hired someone, and she'd tell me my original listing images were fine. I second-guessed everything.

What did it cost me? (time, money, energy)

- Money: $15,000+ in program fees
- Time: 6-8 hours daily playing around and "trying" to implement everything
- Energy: Complete burnout, health issues from stress, joy for business completely disappeared

Why didn't it work? I didn't understand that I had to master the basics first—just like in Karate Kid, where he had to focus on the fundamentals before learning the advanced moves. I didn't fully commit. I exhibited self-sabotage behavior due to lack of faith in myself and the process. I was in a rush to see results instead of trusting the timeline. I just wasn't coachable at that time. Instead of focusing on one thing until successful, I continued to purchase other coaches or products to "fill in the gaps," which only created more confusion and scattered my focus even further.

What did I learn from it? I learned that no matter how much you pay for a program, you have to actually do the work to see if it will work. You have to let go—or work hard on letting go of something—so that your hands are free to grab something else. Your business will shine a light on all your insecurities, and that's how progress is made. I learned that before you get the progress, you have to go through the process. I also learned that I need to master the basics first before moving to advanced strategies, and that being coachable means following through completely, not just cherry-picking what feels comfortable. Most importantly, I learned that my scattered focus and constant search for the "next thing" was actually self-sabotage disguised as productivity.

How will I use this lesson going forward? Now when I see new programs or opportunities, I ask myself: "Have I completed any of my other programs in their entirety? If the answer is no, it's not the program—I am the problem. Let me fix me first so that I can follow a program and see results." I've learned to resist the urge to buy more solutions when what I really need is to execute what I already have. I focus on mastering one thing at a time, taking baby steps instead of trying to rush the process. I also practice letting go of what's not working so I can fully commit to what could work.

When Investment Doesn't Equal Commitment

This wasn't just a business mistake; it was a mirror. I kept telling myself that I just needed the *right* strategy, the *right* program, the *right* coach. But the truth was, I didn't need more information; I needed more commitment to the basics and more trust in myself.

Paying a lot doesn't mean you'll show up. Confusion isn't always a lack of clarity—it's sometimes a lack of decision. I had one foot in and one foot out, trying to keep old systems alive while hoping something new would rescue me.

But no program can do the work for you. That's the difference between buying help and being coachable, between watching a module and changing your behavior. Looking back, that $15K wasn't wasted—it was the tuition I paid to finally learn what it means to go all in. Not all in on a program—but all in on *me*.

Let's look at what the **Simple Format** looks like in real life. This next example may seem small, but it's proof that powerful insights often come from everyday decisions—not just major failures.

Simple Format Example: The $1,000 Digital Product Purchase

Date of failure: May-July 2024

Date of reflection: December 15, 2024

What happened? I spent $1,000 on digital products that I never added to my shop because I was in a failing state. Completely overwhelmed and unable to keep up with what I was buying. The products just sat unused while I continued purchasing more. I had been failing for quite some time, even when I was seeing success in my shops, because I wasn't celebrating any wins or recognizing my progress.

What did I learn? I should only purchase new products after I've uploaded the ones I already have. I need to spend more time researching before buying instead of impulse purchasing. Most importantly, I gained the confidence to listen to myself and trust my instincts about when I'm taking on too much. I also learned that success without acknowledgment feels like failure and that celebrating wins is crucial for maintaining a healthy business mindset.

How do I use that lesson now? I have a "one in, one out" rule— I don't buy new digital products until I've fully utilized what I already own. I also pay attention to my mental state before making purchases and ask myself: "Am I buying this from a place of strategy or overwhelm?" When I'm feeling scattered, I pause on new purchases until I'm back in a clear headspace. Most importantly, I now regularly celebrate my wins, no matter how small, to maintain perspective and motivation.

Why the Simple Format Still Hits Deep

This example might seem small, but it reflects something major: we often confuse momentum with progress. I was buying digital products because I felt like I was *doing* something—but in reality, I was just avoiding the discomfort of implementation.

It also reminded me that sometimes success and failure happen at the same time. I had shops that were generating sales, but because I wasn't stopping to celebrate those wins, it felt like I was failing. I was chasing the next milestone without recognizing how far I'd come.

That's why the Simple Format matters just as much as the deeper dives. The insights may come from smaller moments, but the impact is real—especially when those lessons are repeated over time.

How to Start Your Failure Portfolio Today

If we want different results, we have to change what we're putting in. That means confronting what we'd rather avoid: our failures. We have been conditioned to move on quickly, to bury the mistakes and pretend they never happened. But if we want a different outcome, we have to release what's been holding us back. And the only way to do that is to begin.

But here's the truth: you already have valuable material. You just need to dig it up and extract the gold.

Step 1: Choose Your Tool

Keep it simple. Your Failure Portfolio doesn't need to be fancy—it needs to be accessible. Choose something you'll actually use:

- A simple notebook you keep on your desk
- A Google Doc you can access from anywhere
- A note in your phone for quick captures
- A dedicated journal just for business lessons

Step 2: Your First Entry (Right Now)

Pick one "failure" from your past year, something that didn't go as planned but taught you something valuable.

Don't overthink it. It doesn't have to be a big business disaster. Maybe it was:

- A social media post that got no engagement
- A price you tested that nobody paid
- A networking event that felt awkward
- A product idea you abandoned
- A collaboration that didn't work out

Choose the format that feels easiest for you: detailed or simple.

Step 3: Build the Habit

The magic happens when this becomes a regular practice, not just a one-time exercise. Here's how to make it stick:

After every experiment: Whether it works or doesn't, capture what you learned. Success teaches you what worked; failure teaches you what to avoid.

Weekly review: Every Friday, ask yourself: "What didn't go as planned this week, and what did I learn from it?"

Monthly pattern recognition: Look back at your entries and ask: "What patterns am I seeing? What keeps coming up?"

Quarterly wisdom extraction: Review your biggest lessons and ask: "How have these insights changed my approach? What would I tell my past self?"

Step 4: Apply What You've Learned

Your Failure Portfolio becomes a powerful tool when you start using it to make decisions. Before you launch something new, revisit what you've documented and ask yourself:

- Have I tried something similar before? What did I learn?
- What patterns from past failures should I watch out for?
- What assumptions am I making that I've been wrong about before?
- How can I structure this experiment to maximize learning, no matter the outcome?

This is how you move from reacting to reflecting—and from guessing to growing.

Common Mistakes When Starting

- Don't wait until you have a "big enough" failure to start. Small setbacks contain valuable lessons too.
- Don't judge your entries or try to make them sound professional. Raw honesty gives you better insights than polished stories.
- Don't skip entries because you are embarrassed. The failures that make you cringe often contain the most valuable lessons.
- Don't expect immediate transformation. Like compound interest, the real power builds over time.

Your Competitive Advantage

Most entrepreneurs hide their failures and repeat their mistakes. You are about to document your failures and transform them into business intelligence.

One documented failure teaches you something about your market. Five documented failures reveal patterns. Ten documented failures make you an expert on what doesn't work, which makes you incredibly valuable to people still trying to figure it out.

Every entry in your Failure Portfolio becomes a competitive advantage because you know something your competitors are still learning the hard way. Six months from now, you'll have insights into your market, your customers, and your own patterns that took me years to discover.

You'll make decisions faster, avoid costly mistakes, and build confidence in your ability to handle whatever comes next. Your failures aren't your shame—they're your secret weapon. It's time to start using them.

Ready to Start Building Your Failure Portfolio Today?

Get my proven Failure Portfolio Templates (FREE) and start extracting gold from your setbacks immediately:

- Ready-to-use templates for both simple and detailed formats
- Quick-start implementation guide
- Bonus examples to get you inspired
- Monthly review worksheet to spot patterns

Download Your FREE Failure Portfolio Guide Now

https://katyyamoses.myflodesk.com/failureportfolio

Scan the QR code or visit the link above to get instant access to your templates.

Stop hiding your failures. Start leveraging them.

Your breakthrough awaits on the other side of the lessons you are hesitant to learn.

PART III

THE FAILURE FRAMEWORK

CHAPTER 7
Do It Scared

Why Fear Is Proof You're on the Right Path

This chapter isn't about strategy. It's about the fear that creeps in right before you take your first big step, and what to do when it shows up louder than your confidence. Fear rarely visits when you're coasting. It shows up at the edge of growth. When something matters, when something might change you, and when part of you is ready even if the rest isn't sure.

Most of us assume fear means stopping. But more often, it's a sign you're heading in the right direction. It doesn't mean you're not qualified. It means you care. It means you're about to stretch. You don't need to wait for clarity or calm. What you need is the willingness to move, even when the next step feels uncertain.

The Day Fear Became My Guide

Let me take you back to the moment that changed everything for me, the day I stopped fighting fear and started following it. Because you don't have to wait for fear to leave the room. You just have to move anyway.

What No One Tells You About Fear

We spend our whole lives being taught how to stay safe, to avoid mistakes, avoid embarrassment, avoid risk. So, when fear shows up, most of us assume it's a stop sign. But in reality, it's often the opposite.

Fear doesn't visit when you're playing small. It doesn't show up when you are following someone else's checklist or walking a well-worn path. Fear appears when something is on the line—when your choices begin to reflect who you really are and what you really want.

What no one tells you about chasing your dreams is this: fear doesn't disappear; it just changes roles. It quietly moves your boldness, your passion, your dreams to the passenger seat, while it grabs the wheel and takes control.

And that's the part we have to notice because fear doesn't always show up as panic. Sometimes it disguises itself as logic, caution, or perfectionism. It talks you out of risk and convinces you that hesitation is wisdom. But often, it's just insecurity in disguise.

Fear isn't always a sign you're doing something wrong. It's often a sign you're finally doing something real. Of course, you're scared. You're making decisions without a syllabus. You're showing up without knowing if anyone will clap. You're moving forward even though there's no grade, no gold star, no guaranteed result.

But that's where the growth is. That's where creativity lives. Not in the comfort of certainty, but in the tension between who you were and who you're becoming.

Fear doesn't disappear when you step into your purpose; it just shifts roles. The question isn't how to get rid of it. The question is: *Can you walk with it without letting it lead?*

The answer is yes. You prove that every time you take one small step, even if your voice shakes and your confidence wavers. You don't need fear to leave the room. You just need to stop giving it the mic.

The Roots of Fear Run Deep

So where does this kind of fear come from?

As a former educator, I started to notice something unsettling, especially in my last few years working in the school system. The fear that holds so many of us back in adulthood—the kind that stops us from starting or growing a business—often begins in childhood.

From a young age, we are trained to look for the right answer, follow directions, and stay inside the lines. We are taught to walk in straight lines, raise our hands, and wait our turn. There's structure, routine, and reward. And while those things help children develop into thoughtful, functioning adults, they also teach that progress is tied to performance. That success only comes with approval.

Our school system is designed to reach the masses: to prepare children for society, for safety, and for stability. And for many, that system works. But for parents seeking to nurture curiosity and creativity, options like Montessori, private education, or homeschooling offer a different approach—one that makes room for exploration, choice, and self-direction.

We don't have to overhaul the entire school system to make this shift. Even simple changes like letting children help with a family business, earn their own money, or make small decisions about how they learn can preserve that creative spark.

Because here's what I saw in the classroom: Over time, that wild, unfiltered creativity—the kind that fuels innovation—gets trained out. We teach kids to master benchmarks, follow directions, and earn gold stars. And eventually, we grow into adults who crave those gold stars without realizing it.

That mindset doesn't translate to entrepreneurship. In business, there's no straight line. No guaranteed grade. No teacher validating your effort. Just uncertainty, trial, and the kind of resilience that school rarely prepares us for.

That realization stayed with me. I wasn't just watching creativity shrink in the classroom; I was living the long-term effects of it in my own life. I knew how to follow rules. I didn't know how to trust myself. And that's why fear shows up so loud when you finally step out on your own. Because you are no longer working for approval. You are working for alignment. And no one hands out a certificate for that.

Scared, Lost, and Uncomfortable: The 3 Amigos of Growth

If you're reading this feeling scared, lost, and uncomfortable about starting a business, congratulations! You're exactly where you're supposed to be.

Scared means you're about to do something significant. Lost means you're entering uncharted territory where real growth happens. Uncomfortable means you're stretching beyond your current capacity.

These feelings aren't signals to turn back; they are confirmation that you're on the right path. I learned this the hard way during my first year as a tax preparer. It was December 2020. I had just finished my second tax preparation program because one wasn't enough. I needed multiple perspectives. I even completed the IRS Annual Filing Season Program. Over $7,000 invested. Certificates hung on my wall like battle scars.

My goal? Earn $20,000 that season. My reality? I was fired up with knowledge and flat broke on clients. When January rolled around, I dabbled. I recorded one video. Maybe two. Updated my bio. Mailed gift packages to teacher friends in other states, hoping they'd post my flyers in their lounges. I offered referral bonuses to anyone who'd listened.

I did everything *except* the one thing that actually mattered: showing up. The excuses came fast:

"Maybe next year I'll try harder."

"I don't have time to get clients."

"I'm too new; who would trust me?"

But beneath all those excuses was the real truth: I was terrified. How could I compete with Enrolled Agents, CPAs, and seasoned pros when I was just a beginner with some certificates? I was scared to go live. Uncomfortable promoting myself. Afraid people would ask questions I couldn't answer—or worse, say no. So, I stayed quiet. Played it safe. And told myself I was "trying."

When the season ended, I had fifteen clients. And I was devastated. Not because fifteen was bad, but because I couldn't see that it was good. I convinced myself I'd failed. I hadn't made my $20K goal. I felt like I'd wasted $7,000 and four months of my life.

After a few years, I went back to what felt safe: teaching. It felt like defeat. Like proof that maybe I wasn't cut out for entrepreneurship. Maybe I had overestimated myself. Maybe I should stick with drafting IEPs and predictable paychecks.

But deep down, I knew the truth: I hadn't really shown up. That was the real reason I didn't hit my goal. I had been targeting the wrong audience while hiding behind the excuse of being "too new."

I finally saw it clearly: those fifteen clients were *miraculous*. Fifteen people trusted a stranger with their most personal financial details. Fifteen people said yes even when I barely showed up. Fifteen people became the foundation for everything that came after.

And looking back, I see now: the 3 Amigos were with me the entire time. I just didn't know they were my allies.

I was scared to go live. That fear meant I was about to do something that mattered. I was lost in marketing strategies, unsure of my audience. That confusion meant I was in a space where growth happens. I was deeply uncomfortable with the vulnerability of building something from scratch. That discomfort was proof I was growing.

The problem wasn't the fear. The problem was thinking those feelings meant I should stop. But those fifteen clients? They came because I moved forward anyway—imperfectly, inconsistently, but forward.

The 3 Amigos don't leave once you start seeing success. They just change costumes. When they show up again dressed as overthinking, hesitation, or "playing it safe," recognize them. Call them what they are. And move forward anyway, not with false confidence, but with clear-eyed faith.

That's why I started journaling my failures. Because the more you document your journey, the easier it becomes to see fear for what it is: a signpost. The more you reflect, the quicker you can tell the difference between wisdom and worry.

The goal isn't to eliminate fear, confusion, or discomfort. The goal is to walk beside them and become the leader. And that's especially important when another visitor shows up—one that doesn't just whisper doubt, but questions your entire identity.

When Imposter Syndrome Knocked on My Door

Even after years of running a successful business, imposter syndrome still finds a way to sneak in—especially when I start something new.

That's what happened when I decided to step outside of Etsy and build my own digital storefront. I had the receipts. I had the results. But stepping into a new environment made me feel like a beginner all over again.

No one was asking for my credentials—but my own mind was.

That's when the 3 Amigos showed up again. Only this time, they had new names: Self-Doubt. Comparison. Imposter Syndrome. They looked different, but the root was the same: fear in disguise. Different costumes, same message: *You're not ready.*

And that's the thing: imposter syndrome doesn't care how much you've already done. It reappears the moment you enter unfamiliar territory. Yes, I'm more aware of it now. I can recognize when those negative thoughts try to take over, telling me I'm not ready, not good enough, or not credible in this new space. But awareness doesn't make the voice disappear. It just gives me the power to respond differently.

Now, when doubt creeps in, I replace it. I remind myself of what's true: Yes, I may be new to this platform. But I am not new to delivering value. I am not new to creating with purpose. I am not new to helping people win.

And that's the pattern most people don't talk about: with every new level, the old doubts resurface just dressed a little differently. That's why learning to spot them is so important. Not so you can avoid them, but so you can walk through them with clarity.

Because once you recognize fear for what it really is, you can finally stop waiting for it to disappear and start learning how to move with it.

Let me show you what that looks like in real life.

Action Despite Fear: How to Move When You Are Terrified

Here's the secret nobody talks about: you don't have to eliminate fear to take action. You just have to take action with fear riding shotgun.

My "Do It Scared" Toolkit:

The 10-Minute Rule: When I'm paralyzed by a big, overwhelming task, I commit to working on it for just 10 minutes. Usually, starting is the hardest part, and momentum takes over. For example, I once sat staring at a blank email draft for hours, afraid to pitch a collaboration. I finally set a timer for 10 minutes to get words down. By the time it dinged, I had written the whole thing and hit send.

The Next Right Step: Instead of trying to see the whole staircase, I focus on just the next step. What's one small thing I can do today to move forward? When leaving teaching felt overwhelming, I didn't focus on "How do I build a six-figure business?" Instead, I asked, "What's one product I can list today?" That single listing led to my first sale, which led to my second, and so on.

The Balance Exercise: I acknowledge what might not work, but then I spend twice as much time writing about what could go beautifully right.

The Support Squad: I surrounded myself with people who believed in my vision, even when I didn't believe in it myself. Their faith carried me through my doubt.

The Evidence File: I save screenshots of good reviews and document small wins. When doubt creeps in, I read these reminders of what's working. Seeing that real people were already benefiting from my work gave me the courage to take the leap. Even if you haven't started a business yet, you've been building skills and helping people your whole life. When doubt creeps in, read these reminders of your existing strengths.

The Courage Journal: I write down what scared me and how I moved forward anyway. Sometimes just documenting my brave moments shows me I'm stronger than I think. Other times, it helps me see patterns in what triggers my fear so I can prepare better next time.

The Beautiful Truth About Courage

Courage isn't the absence of fear; it's feeling the fear and doing it anyway. It's not about being fearless; it's about being fear-full and moving forward regardless.

Every successful entrepreneur I know has a story about the moment they did something that terrified them: the day they quit their job, launched their first product, raised their prices, or put themselves out there in a way that felt impossibly vulnerable.

Fear evolves. It may look different at each stage, but it still shows up. First, you're afraid to start. Then, you're afraid to scale. Then, to hire. Then, to expand. Fear is just the price of admission to the life you really want.

Your Scared, Beautiful Beginning

There are two types of people with business dreams: entrepreneurs and "wonderpreneurs." The difference isn't talent or resources—it's the willingness to act despite fear.

Entrepreneurs feel the terror and move forward anyway. Wonderpreneurs wonder if they're ready, wonder if it's the right time, wonder if they have what it takes, and stay stuck in the wondering.

Every successful business owner I know has felt exactly what you are feeling right now. The fear doesn't disqualify you; it confirms you are on to something meaningful.

The difference between those who succeed and those who stay stuck isn't the absence of fear—it's the willingness to do it scared. If you wander into entrepreneurship, you cannot stay there long. You have to choose a side: be all in or step aside.

Your fear is a compass pointing toward your growth. Start where you are. Use what you have. Do what you can. And when fear tries to convince you to wait until you are ready, remember this: Ready is a myth. Courage is a choice.

If you've helped even 1-2 people succeed—friends, family, colleagues—you are already walking the path of an expert. No one begins as one. Expertise grows through action.

You have knowledge that people are searching for. You have gifts that can change lives.

Are you still in wonderland?

The business you're meant to build lives on the other side of fear. And the only way to reach it is to walk through.

Exactly as you are. Scared. Brave. Becoming.

Here's a challenge:
Write down one thing that frightens you about starting your business—just one.
Then, write down the smallest step you can take toward it today. Not tomorrow. Not next week. Today.

That's it. Begin there. Your courage is calling. And the life you've been dreaming of is waiting on the other side of your first brave step.

CHAPTER 8
My Business, My Baby

I'll never forget watching each of my kids take their first steps. My oldest was cautious and calculated; my middle child was fearless and headstrong; and my youngest observed and joined in one morning as if she had been walking for weeks. Different paths, same beautiful destination.

My oldest was methodical, cruising along furniture for weeks, occasionally letting go for a wobbly second before landing on his diaper-cushioned bottom. He studied every step and calculated every risk.

My middle child was fearless; one day she let go and stumbled forward as if walking was the most natural thing in the world, even though she face-planted after three steps.

My youngest watched her siblings and seemed to think, "If they can do it..." and just started walking one morning as if she had been doing it all along.

Three kids, three completely different approaches, but the same beautiful result. Just like them, my business needed time, its own pace, and encouragement at every stage—because building a business is a lot like raising a baby.

Starting my business felt exactly the same. For months, I had been "cruising," holding onto the security of my teaching job while testing small digital products on the side. Occasionally, I'd hear, "You are so good with kids; why do you want to stop doing this?" I would respond, "I don't want to teach kids ABCs; I want to help their parents learn about 123s." Finance and taxes are my passion.

But just like my kids' first steps, my business breakthrough didn't occur because I forced it. It happened because I allowed it time to develop, protected it when it was vulnerable, and celebrated every wobbly step forward.

Your business is your baby. And just like raising a child, there are no shortcuts to healthy development.

The Patience Principle: Why Businesses Need Time to "Walk"

My oldest son was walking at nine months, which was perfectly normal. What fascinated me was watching his process. He was scared at first. You could see the hesitation on his little face. So, he devised his own strategy: using his ride-and-push toy car for confidence. The scariest part was getting started. But after that initial fear, he was walking all over the house as if he had been doing it forever.

What I didn't realize back then—while watching my kids take their first steps—was that those moments would later mirror the milestones in my business. It wasn't until I started reflecting on my own journey, especially the failures, that this connection became clear.

I often see new entrepreneurs trying to force their three-month-old businesses to run marathons. They compare their startup to someone else's established company and panic that they're behind. They push for results before the foundation is solid and then wonder why everything feels unstable.

Your business has developmental stages, just like a baby:

The Crawling Stage (Months 1-6): You are moving, but slowly. Every inch forward is hard work. You are building basic skills: learning to create products, understanding your customers, and figuring out operations. This isn't failure; this is development.

The Cruising Stage (Months 6-12): You are gaining confidence but still need support. You might have some sales, a few customers, and some systems in place. You are holding onto "furniture"—perhaps keeping your day job or relying on other income sources. This isn't playing it safe; this is being smart.

The First Steps Stage (Year 1-2): Wobbly but walking. You are making real money, but it's inconsistent. Some days you feel like a true entrepreneur; other days you wonder what you are doing. This isn't imposter syndrome; this is normal.

The Running Stage (Year 2+): Confident movement toward your goals. You are not just surviving; you are thriving. But even now, you'll occasionally stumble. That's not regression; that's life.

I spent my first year expecting my business to run while it was still learning to crawl. The frustration nearly extinguished my entrepreneurial spirit. It wasn't until I embraced the patience principle that everything changed.

What changed when I stopped pushing:

- I celebrated small wins instead of dismissing them.
- I focused on building skills rather than chasing revenue.
- I invested in systems instead of shortcuts.
- I measured progress in learning, not just earning.

Once I stopped forcing my business to grow faster, it actually began to grow more quickly. I was working with its natural development instead of against it.

Protecting vs. Pushing: When to Nurture and When to Challenge

The hardest part of raising my kids and my business has been knowing when to protect and when to push. Protect too much, and growth stagnates. Push too hard, and confidence shatters.

With my kids, I learned that protection looks like baby-proofing the house so they can explore safely, not carrying them everywhere so they never fall. Pushing means encouraging them to try the monkey bars, not forcing them to do soccer and ballet before they can walk.

In business, protection means:

- Keeping your day job until your business income is stable.
- Setting boundaries around your time and energy.
- Building emergency funds instead of reinvesting every penny.
- Starting with low-risk experiments before making big investments—for example, instead of launching a full course, I tested the waters with a $27 bundle.

- Surrounding yourself with supportive people during vulnerable phases.

In business, pushing means:

- Raising your prices when you are undercharging—I remember my stomach churning as I changed my rates, but clients paid without hesitation, showing me I'd been undervaluing myself for too long.
- Putting yourself out there even when it feels scary.
- Having difficult conversations with clients or partners.
- Building your own platform instead of relying solely on marketplace traffic—eventually moving from depending on Etsy's algorithm to creating your own website and email list.
- Investing in growth when the foundation is solid.
- Taking calculated risks that align with your goals.

The mistake I made early on was thinking protection meant playing small and pushing meant risking everything. Neither was true.

The turning point came when I saw that I could protect my well-being while being bold with my business decisions. I could nurture my confidence while challenging my comfort zone.

Here's how I learned to balance protection and pushing:

When my business was in its **crawling stage**, I protected my energy by not taking on clients who drained me, but I pushed myself to create content consistently even when no one seemed to be listening.

When my business started **walking**, I protected my family time by setting strict boundaries, but I pushed myself to raise my prices even though it felt terrifying.

When my business was ready to **run**, I protected my existing Etsy income while pushing myself to build my own website and email list, creating independence from marketplace algorithms.

When my business **took off**, I protected my momentum by saying no to shiny opportunities that didn't fit my goals, but I pushed myself to invest in systems that would support growth.

The key was learning to read my business's developmental stage and respond appropriately, just as I learned to read my children's cues.

Growth Stages:
The Natural Progression Nobody Talks About

Business development isn't linear, it's not predictable, and it definitely doesn't follow the timelines you see in success stories.

Just as some babies walk at nine months and others at fifteen months (both perfectly normal), some businesses hit their stride in year one while others take three years to find their footing. My son completely skipped crawling because he didn't want his knees touching the floor; instead, he bent over and walked on his hands and feet like a little bear. He didn't do that for long; he just started walking upright one day based on a strategy that worked for him. The timeline doesn't determine the outcome.

If the first metaphor is about your baby learning to walk, the next one reflects their school years—each level builds on the last, introducing new lessons and greater independence. Just as children experience predictable developmental stages (even if the timing varies), businesses have growth stages that every entrepreneur must navigate.

Stage 1: The Survival Stage (Everything is New and Hard)
You are figuring out the basics: What do I sell? Who wants to buy it? How do I find customers? How do I deliver value? This stage feels overwhelming because every detail requires conscious thought and effort.

What it looks like: You are Googling "how to write an invoice" and feeling like everyone else received a business manual you missed. You celebrate your first sale as if you won the lottery (because you essentially did).

What you need: Patience with the learning curve, recognition of small wins, and protection from comparisons with more established businesses.

Stage 2: The Systems Stage (Building the Foundation) You have grasped the basics, but everything is held together with duct tape and determination. You are establishing real systems, processes, and consistency.

What it looks like: You have regular customers, somewhat predictable income, and actual business processes. However, you are still the bottleneck for everything, and scaling feels impossible. In business terms, a "bottleneck" means you are the one slowing everything down—not because you are doing something wrong, but because nothing can move forward without your input. That makes growth feel frustratingly out of reach.

What you need: Investment in tools and systems, boundaries around your time, and patience with the messy middle of growth.

Stage 3: The Scale Stage (Momentum Builds) Your systems are functioning, your message is clear, and growth feels more natural than forced. You are not just surviving; you are building something sustainable.

What it looks like: Referrals start coming in regularly, people recognize your expertise, and you can take a day off without everything collapsing.

What you need: Continued investment in what's working, strategic risk-taking for growth, and safeguarding the culture and values that got you here.

Stage 4: The Mastery Stage (It Finally Feels Natural) Business feels less like a challenge and more like a skill you have honed. You have developed instincts, confidence, and sustainable systems.

What it looks like: You make decisions quickly because you understand your market, your customers trust your recommendations, and new challenges feel manageable rather than overwhelming.

What you need: Ongoing evolution, strategic partnerships, and a safeguard against complacency.

The plot twist: You will cycle through mini-versions of these stages every time you launch something new, enter a new market, or scale to a new level. Each time gets easier because you understand the process, but it still requires patience with development.

At the time of writing this, I'm in Stage 3 with my main business but back in Stage 1 with my YouTube channel. Instead of feeling frustrated, I'm excited. I know what comes next, and I understand how to navigate each stage effectively.

Celebrating Small Wins: Why Every Step Forward Matters

When my kids took their first independent steps, I didn't think, "Well, they should have been doing this months ago," or, "This doesn't count until they can run a marathon." I celebrated each step like they just won an Olympic gold medal because, in their world, they had.

But when my business reached small milestones, my inner critic scoffed: "$100? That's pocket change. Fifty subscribers? That's nothing. One testimonial? You are hardly credible." Yet, every win told a different story—and it was worth listening to.

The problem with dismissing small wins isn't just that it kills your motivation (though it does). The real issue is that small wins compound into big victories, but only if you acknowledge and build on them.

Every small win in my business created momentum for the next level:

My first $10 sale taught me that people would actually pay for what I created. Without that lesson, I never would have raised my prices to $100.

My first $100 sale showed me I could deliver real value at a higher price point. Without that confidence, I never would have created my $400 offering.

The celebration practice that changed everything: Instead of waiting for "big" achievements to celebrate, I started treating business milestones like childhood milestones—acknowledging that each stage of development deserves recognition.

Baby Milestone	Business Milestone
First word	First sale
First sentence	First month of consistent income
First playdate	First client testimonial
First steps	First profitable month
Running confidently	Consistent growth and systems

When you frame it this way, celebrating becomes natural rather than feeling self-indulgent.

Small wins I celebrate now:

- Completing a project on time (even if it's small)
- Receiving positive feedback (even from one person)
- Solving a customer problem (even if it's simple)
- Learning something new (even if it seems basic)
- Taking action despite fear (even if the action is tiny)

These celebrations aren't about lowering standards; they're about recognizing that sustainable success is built on a foundation of acknowledged progress.

The Long Game: Building Businesses That Last

The biggest difference between businesses that survive their first few years and those that don't isn't talent, luck, or even initial success. It's the founder's ability to play the long game—to build something that can weather multiple cycles of failure and keep growing.

Just like raising a child, building a business requires thinking beyond immediate challenges to long-term development. You are not just trying to get through today; you are creating something that will thrive for years.

This long-term thinking requires a fundamental shift in how you approach every aspect of your business.

The Mindset Shift

The biggest breakthrough in my business didn't come from a new strategy or tool—it came from changing how I thought about growth itself.

From: "I need to make money this month"
To: "I need to build systems that will generate consistent revenue"

From: "I need this launch to be perfect"
To: "I need to learn from this launch to improve the next one"

From: "I need to work harder"
To: "I need to work more strategically"

From: "I need to do everything myself"
To: "I need to create a business that can run without me"

This shift didn't happen overnight for me. It occurred gradually as I observed some entrepreneur friends burn out while others built sustainable success.

Burnout vs. Sustainability

I've seen this pattern play out countless times: two entrepreneurs start with similar dreams, similar skills, and similar circumstances. Five years later, one has burned out and quit, while the other has built a thriving, sustainable business. Here's the difference:

The friend who burned out:

- Measured success only in immediate revenue
- Worked unsustainable hours to hit short-term goals
- Neglected systems and relationships for quick wins
- Took every setback as evidence they weren't cut out for business

I watched one friend pour everything into a viral product launch—70-hour weeks, maxed-out credit cards, and promises to family that "this will be the one." When the launch flopped, she was so emotionally and financially drained that she shut down her entire business and returned to her corporate job.

The friend who built lasting businesses:

- Measured success in learning and systems-building
- Worked consistently but sustainably
- Invested in relationships and infrastructure even when it didn't pay off immediately
- Treated setbacks as data for improving their approach

Another friend took a completely different approach. She spent her first year making maybe $200 a month while building systems, nurturing relationships, and learning from every small experiment. Three years later, she runs a six-figure business that supports her entire family, and she works fewer hours than she did in her corporate job.

These stories illustrate the contrast perfectly: one approach burns bright and fast, while the other builds steadily and sustainably. The difference wasn't talent or luck; it was strategy and mindset.

What Made the Difference

So what actually helped me grow? It wasn't luck, and it definitely wasn't hustle alone. When I looked back, five key shifts stood out—choices I made on purpose that helped me build something sustainable, not just successful.

Investment in Learning: Instead of spending every dollar on ads or tools, I invested in courses, books, and mentorship that would compound over time.

Relationship Building: Instead of just focusing on transactions, I built genuine relationships with customers, peers, and mentors.

System Creation: Instead of simply hustling harder, I established repeatable processes that could scale without burning me out.

Value Consistency: Instead of chasing trends, I focused on consistently delivering value in my unique way.

Personal Sustainability: Instead of sacrificing everything for business growth, I created a business that enhanced my life rather than consumed it.

The result? A business that survived my learning curve, multiple economic uncertainties, and significant life changes. It wasn't immediately successful, but it was built to last.

Your Business Is Learning to Walk

Your business doesn't need to sprint before it's ready. Like a child, it needs strength, balance, and confidence—developed slowly, through stages, not pressure.

Give your business what every healthy baby needs:

- Time to develop at its natural pace
- Protection from unnecessary risks during vulnerable stages
- Challenges that promote growth without overwhelming the system
- Celebration of every developmental milestone
- Patience with the messy, non-linear process of growth

Every business you admire once had a shaky beginning. They all had crawling phases. They all fell down. What made them different wasn't luck or talent; it was how gently they were supported and how consistently they were nurtured through their early years.

Your business is learning to walk. That means progress will be slow, unsteady, and sometimes invisible. But step by step, you're getting closer to something remarkable.

Soon, you will look up and realize your business isn't just walking; it's running toward success. And when that day comes, you will know it didn't happen overnight. It happened because you honored the process.

So for now, celebrate every inch forward. Protect what you are building. Trust what's taking root.

Your baby's first steps are coming—and they are going to be beautiful.

CHAPTER 9

The Power of the Feedback Loop

What Is a Feedback Loop—and Why It Matters

In business, a feedback loop is the ongoing cycle of listening to your audience, responding to what they say, and making improvements based on what you learn. It's not just about collecting opinions; it's about using customer responses to guide your decisions, improve your products, and grow your business with intention. When done right, this loop becomes your greatest tool for progress.

The most valuable business education I've ever received didn't come from courses or books. It came from customers telling me exactly what I was doing wrong and right. Here's how feedback became my secret weapon.

Customers as Teachers: The Classroom I Never Expected

As a special education teacher, I had to constantly adapt based on each student's individual needs. Every day was about reading cues, modifying approaches, and discovering what actually worked for each child.

Then I became an entrepreneur, and my customers became my most brutal and most valuable teachers.

The lessons they taught me were nothing like what I expected:

Here are three surprising truths my customers shared that reshaped my entire approach.

Lesson 1: What I think they need and what they actually need are often completely different.

I started offering financial planning consultations where I would analyze their budgets, show them how to increase their income, and create plans for starting a business or side hustle to offset their tax liability. I was excited about these comprehensive strategies that could transform their entire financial picture.

People would get excited during our sessions, but most didn't follow through with the plans I provided. The feedback was enlightening: "The budget help was exactly what I needed, but starting a business feels overwhelming right now."

They wanted help organizing their current finances, not a complete financial overhaul. The side hustle strategy—even though it could save them significant money on taxes—was too much, too soon. They needed to master their basic budget before they could handle entrepreneurial tax strategies.

Lesson 2: The problems they're willing to pay to solve aren't always the problems they complain about most.

Teachers often complained about difficult students, yet they wouldn't pay for behavior management courses. They rarely mentioned feeling financially trapped, but they'd pay premium prices for anything that promised financial freedom.

The pain they discuss and the pain they will invest in solving are two different things.

Lesson 3: How they describe their problems and how I describe their solutions need to match exactly.

I kept talking about "building wealth" and "financial literacy." They kept saying they wanted to "stop living paycheck to paycheck" and "have breathing room." Same goal, completely different language.

When I started using their words instead of my expert terminology, everything changed.

The customer feedback that transformed my business:

"I don't need another budget spreadsheet. I need someone to tell me it's okay to spend money on coffee if it makes me happy."

This taught me that my customers needed permission and emotional support, not just practical tools.

"Your story about crying in your car over money stress made me feel seen. Do you have more resources for people like me?"

This taught me that vulnerability and relatability were more valuable than credentials and expertise.

"I tried to implement everything you taught, but I got overwhelmed and quit. Can you break this down into smaller steps?"

This taught me that sustainable change happens in baby steps, not giant leaps.

Each feedback moment felt like a student raising their hand with an unexpected question. My job wasn't to repeat the lesson; it was to meet them where they were learning. Instead of getting frustrated that they weren't absorbing what I was teaching, I adjusted my lessons based on what they were actually trying to learn.

The mindset shift that changed everything: I stopped trying to educate my market and started learning from my market. This was especially crucial in the beginning stage, when I had more theories than real experience, and every customer interaction taught me something I couldn't have learned any other way.

Failing Fast and Cheap: My $50 Experiment Strategy

The issue with my early business failures wasn't that they happened; it was that they were expensive and slow. I'd spend months and hundreds of dollars creating something before discovering it wasn't what people wanted.

Then I discovered the magic of failing fast and cheap, and everything changed.

The $50 Experiment Rule

Here's the approach I wish I had used earlier—and what I recommend you try: Before you invest significant time or money in any business idea, test it with a maximum budget of $50 and a maximum timeline of two weeks.

But if you are a complete beginner, start even smaller:

Beginner Validation ($0-$20)

Start with free validation:

- Post questions in Facebook groups where your target audience hangs out
- Ask friends/family about problems they'd pay to solve
- Look at what questions people are asking in online communities
- Check what products are selling on platforms like Etsy or Amazon

Then, test tiny ($10-20):

- Create a simple survey using Google Forms
- Test headlines or product ideas on social media
- Buy a competitor's low-priced product to understand what customers want

$50 Test Ideas

Testing demand for a new service: Instead of creating the entire offering first, write a compelling description and post it in a Facebook group, asking, "Would you be interested in this? What questions would you want it to answer?" Another approach is to test small services with your current audience—I started offering custom message cards in my existing Etsy shop to discover what my customers were actually looking for, which led me to uncover the demand for bereavement cards I never knew existed.

Testing Price Points: Instead of guessing what people will pay, test in real time with small offerings. I started offering custom message cards as a service in my Etsy shop for $7. When people kept purchasing the $5 sale price ones instead, I adjusted my pricing and learned what customers valued. This also revealed what types of cards people actually wanted—like bereavement cards, which I hadn't even considered creating.

Testing Content Format Preferences: Instead of assuming people want one type of deliverable, offer the same solution in different formats and let people choose their preference.

For example, with my message card service: I could have tested whether customers preferred:

- Pre-made card templates they could customize themselves
- Completely custom cards designed from scratch
- Semi-custom cards where they choose from design options
- Digital delivery vs. physical cards

Or for any service: You might test whether clients want:

- One comprehensive session vs. multiple shorter sessions
- Written reports vs. video explanations of your recommendations
- Group coaching vs. one-on-one support
- Live calls vs. recorded content accessible anytime

Why Cheap Experiments Work

The beauty of cheap experiments lies in their low risk: when they "fail," you've only lost a small amount of money and two weeks.

When they succeed, you validate demand before committing significant resources.

My Favorite Low-Cost Success Story

My biggest success with cheap experiments occurred in a new tax professional group where confusion about hiring your kids was rampant. I kept encountering the same questions repeatedly and found myself answering them often. Recognizing an opportunity, I began developing a "Hire Your Kids" tax strategy guide.

This $0 observation of recurring questions led to a successful product launch and taught me that the best business ideas stem from genuinely listening to what people seek help with.

The Mindset Shift

Rather than asking, "Will this work?" I began to ask, "What's the cheapest way to find out if this will work?"

For example, instead of spending months creating a full course on tax planning, I could offer a $49 one-hour consultation to test demand. Within a week or so, I would know exactly what my market wanted—and what they didn't.

This approach eliminated analysis paralysis, as the cost of testing was minimal. It also reduced the fear of failure; even 'failed' experiments yielded valuable data for under $50.

Pivot vs. Persevere: The Art of Strategic Course Correction

The most challenging aspect of gathering feedback is not simply collecting it; it's knowing how to act on it. Should you pivot based on one customer's suggestion, or should you persevere through initial rejection because you believe in your vision? How do you differentiate between valuable feedback and random noise?

I learned this lesson the hard way through my Etsy business, where I had to decide whether to trust my vision or listen to customer feedback that challenged it.

The Pivot That's Teaching Me About Listening to Feedback:

After making over 13,000 sales on Etsy, customers frequently asked me, "Do you have an email list I can join?" and "Why are you still on Etsy? You could make more money with your own shop."

Initially, I dismissed these comments. Etsy was working; why fix what wasn't broken?

However, after hearing dozens of customers inquire about email lists and direct access, I realized they were conveying something important: I needed more than Etsy. They craved a deeper connection with me and my work.

How I Pivoted Strategically:

Instead of abandoning Etsy entirely, I decided to create my own online store to showcase my work, grow an email list, and assist others. My Etsy business continues to generate sales, but my presence there has diminished.

This strategic pivot involved three key elements:

- Creating my own online store with full control over my brand
- Developing new products specifically for my store
- Focusing on attracting traffic and customers directly to me instead of relying on Etsy

The Result: I'm still building my online store while maintaining my successful Etsy presence. This pivot allows me to grow an email list, showcase my work more effectively, and establish direct relationships with customers who value my expertise.

What I Learned About When to Pivot vs. Persevere:

One of the hardest decisions in business isn't getting started; it's knowing when to change direction. Every entrepreneur hits a point where something feels off. Maybe sales stall, customers ask for more than you offer, or your strategy starts to feel limiting. That's when the questions begin: Should I switch things up? Stay the course? Is this resistance a sign to push harder—or a signal that it's time to evolve?

I've wrestled with these questions myself. And over time, I've learned this: Growth isn't just about effort. It's about discernment. The most successful business owners don't blindly push through every challenge; they know when to pivot and when to persevere.

Here's how I learned to tell the difference:

Pivot When:

- Multiple customers provide the same feedback about their desires
- You identify consistent opportunities for expansion (like needing YouTube for your videos)
- People love what you do and seek more than your current platform allows
- You find yourself successful but feel constrained by your current approach

Persevere When:

- Your current strategy is effective and yielding consistent results
- Feedback is mixed or contradictory
- You are achieving positive outcomes from your existing efforts
- The risk of change outweighs potential benefits

The Key Insight: Pivoting isn't about abandoning what works. It's about building on it. You can retain successful elements while introducing new ways to serve your customers and grow your business.

My Product Failures: When Flops Became Features

Let me reveal my real product experiences and how each has taught me invaluable lessons about business. I've learned that there are no failed products, only successful market research.

Product I Never Finished

I started researching a comprehensive step-by-step guide for setting up business bank accounts. After spending hours diving into different options, I realized the overwhelming complexity: there are dozens of physical and virtual banks, each with different requirements, fees, and benefits. What seemed like a straightforward guide became an impossible puzzle. There's no one-size-fits-all solution when someone in California might benefit from a completely different bank than someone in Texas, or when a service-based business has different needs than an e-commerce business.

What I Learned: I cannot create a truly helpful product when the variables are too complex to address comprehensively. Even though it would have been valuable, some "great" product ideas are actually too intricate to execute well without overwhelming customers. The research wasn't wasted—it taught me to validate not just demand, but feasibility before diving deep into product creation.

The Feedback Loop: Sometimes the market teaches you through the research process itself. This wasn't a product failure; it was a reminder that even valuable ideas need to be executable to truly serve customers.

E-books That Took Time to Sell

I have several e-books that didn't sell until their second year. I cannot explain the logic behind it, but I believed most of them were good; my customers just didn't see it initially.

One book, aimed at individuals with service-based businesses wanting to promote offline, struggled to gain traction. After noticing low sales, I redesigned the entire e-book, which led to a few sales. However, I realized my target audience in that shop simply wasn't interested in offline advertising.

What I Learned: Sometimes it's not about timing; it's about audience fit. The right product in the wrong market won't sell, regardless of its quality.

The Feedback Loop: My customers taught me this lesson through their silence. Low sales weren't necessarily a reflection of poor content. They were data about market fit. Instead of continuing to push offline advertising to an audience that preferred digital strategies, I learned to pay attention to what my existing customers were actually buying and asking about.

The Pattern in All My Experiences

I learned that success isn't solely about creating good products; it's about understanding your audience, promoting effectively, and not allowing past projects to dictate your future capabilities.

Building Feedback Systems: What I've Learned

The biggest insight I've gained in my business is the need to stop waiting for feedback and start systematically collecting it.

How I Now Use Data to Make Product Decisions: I base my understanding on concrete data, such as the number of likes a product receives, the number of purchases, and especially customer feedback. While no one enjoys negative feedback, it serves as valid data that reveals important insights. If multiple customers express the same concern, it likely indicates a product issue.

Real Example: I had an inexpensive course that initially received positive feedback. However, I later received negative feedback about its lack of value and actionable steps. Consequently, I reviewed the course and created a supplemental guide. I reached out to individuals who left negative reviews and those who contacted me directly. Despite the guide, people still disliked the product, prompting me to remove it from my shop.

What I Learned: Sometimes, the kindest action you can take for your customers and your business is to stop selling something that isn't working, even after attempting to fix it. Poor products damage your reputation more than removing them affects your income.

Simple Feedback Systems I'm Implementing:

1. Paying Attention to What Sells: I'm learning to track which Etsy products attract the most favorites, views, and sales. This informs me about what truly draws my customers, as opposed to what I believe they should want.

2. Reading Customer Messages Carefully: When customers ask questions or offer comments, I'm beginning to identify patterns. For instance, when multiple individuals inquire about email lists or YouTube channels, that indicates what they want from me.

3. Noticing Which Content Gets Responses: I pay attention to which social media posts or messages garner the most engagement. These topics reveal what resonates with my audience.

4. Learning from What Doesn't Sell: Instead of merely moving on from unsold products, I'm striving to understand why. Sometimes it's the audience; other times it's timing or presentation.

5. Asking Direct Questions: When uncertain, I'm learning to directly ask my customers—like posting in groups to gauge interest before creating something.

What I'm Discovering: The feedback is already there; I just need to improve my ability to recognize it and act upon it.

The Mindset Shift I'm Making: Instead of creating what I think people need, I'm learning to develop what they are already indicating they want.

The Revolution That Started with Honest Feedback

I received feedback from a customer that transformed my approach to product improvement. She expressed disappointment with one of my products but hesitated to leave a negative review due to the effort I had invested. She explained that she found the product's organization lacking.

Understanding her perspective, I redesigned the product. Since it was less than a month old, I contacted every customer who had purchased it to inform them about the update. The customer who had initially complained, along with another buyer, both left me 5-star reviews after the redesign.

This experience taught me a crucial lesson: there were likely others who shared her sentiments but didn't voice their concerns. One person's courage to provide honest feedback allowed me to enhance the product for all.

The feedback loop revolution isn't about constantly changing direction. It's about staying connected to the people you serve.

Sometimes feedback prompts a pivot; other times, it encourages perseverance. It can also reveal that what you thought was effective could be even better with minor adjustments.

The Most Important Lesson: Your customers aren't just purchasing your products. They are teaching you how to build a business that truly serves them. The real question isn't whether you will receive feedback; it's whether you will listen, learn, and let it guide you toward the success you both seek.

Every product challenge is merely an expensive lesson if you don't learn from it. However, when you heed feedback and act on it, each interaction becomes valuable market research that improves your next offer. Ultimately, my customers became the coaches I never hired—guiding every pivot, product, and breakthrough. The revolution begins the moment you realize your customers aren't critics; they're your co-creators.

PART IV

PRACTICAL FAILURE STRATEGIES

CHAPTER 10

The 30-Day Failure Challenge

I stared at my journal on a rainy Tuesday morning in March, writing the words that would change everything: "Day 1: I'm going to fail on purpose for the next 30 days."

It sounds crazy, right? Who sets out to fail deliberately? But after months of playing it safe, sticking to my comfortable teaching routine while my entrepreneurial dreams collected dust, I realized something profound: my fear of failure was the very thing preventing my success.

I designed what I called my 30-Day Failure Challenge. Not because I wanted to fail, but because I wanted to become comfortable with the possibility of failure so it would stop controlling my decisions.

Here's the key mindset shift that makes this work: when you give yourself permission to fail, you also give yourself permission to succeed. Most people avoid taking action because they're terrified of not getting it right the first time. But what if "not getting it right" was the whole point? What if failure became your teacher instead of your enemy?

Strategic failure isn't about sloppiness; it's about thoughtful trial, bold attempts, and extracting insights from every result. It's the difference between failing by default and failing on purpose.

We all encounter failure in business; we just need a strategy to embrace it. Failure is beneficial because it helps us improve by practicing. But here's the important distinction: I'm not talking about failing because you skipped the obvious steps. If you want to grow your Instagram to 20K followers but have never posted anything, that's not a valuable failure—that's just neglecting the work. There's nothing to learn there because the answer is clear.

I'm referring to strategic failures where you try something, give it your best effort, and learn from the outcome. Like posting consistently for 30 days and discovering that your audience prefers behind-the-scenes content over polished graphics. That's a failure that teaches you something valuable about your market.

The challenge creates a safe space where you can experiment, learn, and grow without the crushing pressure of needing to be perfect. When you see failure as valuable data rather than personal defeat, everything changes.

What happened over those 30 days didn't just transform my business—it changed my entire relationship with risk, growth, and possibility.

Why 30 Days Change Everything

There's something magical about committing to anything for exactly 30 days. It's long enough to create real change, yet short enough that your brain doesn't panic and sabotage you before you start.

When I decided to "embrace failure" for 30 days, something shifted immediately. Instead of avoiding anything that might not work perfectly, I started seeking opportunities to test, experiment, and learn.

The mindset shift occurred on Day 3. I posted something on social media that I thought might flop, and when it received only two likes, instead of feeling embarrassed, I felt... curious. What could I learn from this? What would work better next time?

That curiosity replaced my usual shame spiral, and everything changed.

Here's what 30 days of intentional "failure" taught me:

Day 5: I tried a new product format that didn't sell. Instead of feeling defeated, I analyzed why and discovered my audience preferred templates over guides.

Day 12: I tested pricing on my Etsy coaching service and uncovered the power of incremental increases. I began offering coaching at $260, and people quickly jumped on it. After completing work for two clients and realizing the value I provided, I raised the price to $365. I lost a potential client who balked at the new rate, but I gained confidence that my work was worth more—and the next client paid the higher rate without question.

Day 18: I expanded from Etsy to my own platform. Sales were slow, but it's new, and I have to build the website, add products, and market. The "failure" taught me that building your own platform takes time, but it's worth starting.

Day 24: I started practicing for my YouTube channel. It felt weird. I practiced in the car while driving, getting comfortable with the awkwardness of talking to a camera.

Day 30: I launched a simple product without overthinking it. The sales were modest, but the time it took to create was a win. Sometimes I have projects that take me 15 hours to create and only sell for $50, making my hourly rate about $3. This simple product took 2 hours and sold for $27, resulting in an effective hourly rate of $13.50—a much better return on my time investment.

The transformation wasn't in the individual outcomes. It was in how I responded to them. Every "failure" became data. Every setback became a setup for something better.

Week 1: Mindset Reset and Failure Audit

The first week isn't about taking big risks or making dramatic changes. It's about honest self-assessment and mental preparation for the journey ahead.

Day 1-2: Your Failure Story Audit. Start by writing down every "failure" you can remember from the past year. Business ideas you didn't pursue, opportunities you passed up, projects you abandoned. Don't judge them—just list them.

Next to each one, write what you learned or what it taught you about yourself, your market, or your goals.

My own audit revealed patterns I hadn't noticed:

- I abandoned projects when they became complicated, not when they stopped working.
- I avoided opportunities that required me to be visible or vulnerable.

- I labeled things "failures" that were actually just incomplete experiments.

This exercise reveals hidden patterns behind your stuck points.

Day 3-4: The Fear Inventory. Write down everything you are afraid might happen if you take more risks in your business. Be specific and dramatic if needed.

Next to each fear, write the realistic worst-case scenario. Most of the time, you will discover your fears are far greater than the actual potential consequences.

This helps you deflate fear by challenging worst-case myths.

Day 5-7: The Success Cost Calculation. This is the hard one. Write down what staying exactly where you are will cost you over the next year. Not just money—consider time, opportunities, growth, and fulfillment.

Often, the cost of inaction is higher than the cost of taking risks. This reminds you that inaction also has a price.

Week 1 Mindset Shifts:

- From "What if this doesn't work?" to "What if this teaches me something valuable?"
- From "I need to avoid mistakes" to "I need to make mistakes faster."
- From "I'm not ready" to "I'll never be ready, and that's okay."

Week 2: Micro-Experiments and Tiny Failures

Week 2 is where the magic begins. You start taking small, intentional actions that might not work and celebrating the learning that comes from each one.

Day 8-10: The $10 Experiment. Choose something you've been considering trying and test it for under $10. Post a question in a Facebook group, create a simple survey, or test a headline or product idea.

The goal isn't success. It's learning. What response do you get? What questions does it raise? What would you do differently next time?

Day 11-12: The Vulnerability Post. Share something authentic on social media—a struggle you are having, a lesson you learned, or a behind-the-scenes moment from your business.

This probably won't "fail," but it might feel scary, which is precisely the point. You are practicing being visible even when you can't control the outcome.

Day 13-14: The Reach-Out Challenge. Contact someone you've been meaning to reach out to but haven't because you are afraid they'll say no or ignore you—a potential collaborator, mentor, or customer.

They might not respond, they might say no, or they might say yes to something amazing. The only way to find out is to ask.

Week 2 Takeaways:

- Most "failures" aren't failures—they're just unexpected outcomes.

- Small experiments build confidence for larger ones.
- People respond better to authenticity than perfection.
- The anticipation of failure is usually worse than the actual experience.

Week 3: Scaling Lessons and Course Corrections

By Week 3, you've built some tolerance for failure and learned from small experiments. Now, it's time to try slightly bigger tests and practice adjusting based on what you learn.

Day 15-17: The Pricing Experiment. Test a higher price on something you sell. Raise your rates for new clients or price a product 20% higher than usual.

You might lose some sales, but you could also discover you've been undervaluing yourself. Either way, you'll learn something about your market and your worth.

Day 18-19: The Platform Expansion Test. Try expanding beyond your current platform or comfort zone. If you only sell on Etsy, create a simple website. If you only post written content, try recording a video (even if it's just for practice).

Sales might be slow at first, or it might feel awkward, but you will learn about building something that's truly yours and expanding your capabilities.

Day 20-21: The Uncomfortable Practice. Practice a skill that feels uncomfortable yet necessary for your business growth. Record yourself explaining your products while talking to a camera in your car. Write a sales email that feels overly "salesy."

The goal isn't perfection—it's becoming comfortable with the discomfort that accompanies growth.

Week 3 Breakthrough Moment: This is typically when individuals experience their most significant mindset shift. You come to realize that "failure" is merely feedback, and feedback is the quickest route to improvement.

What Week 3 taught me:

- Your first platform doesn't have to be your only one.
- Building something new takes time; slow progress is still progress.
- Getting comfortable with discomfort is a skill you can develop.
- Course corrections are part of the process, not signs of failure.

Week 4: Integration and Momentum Building

The final week focuses on taking everything you've learned and establishing sustainable systems for ongoing growth and experimentation.

Day 22-24: The Simple Product Launch. Launch something new without overthinking it. Prioritize speed over perfection. Create a straightforward digital product or service offering that takes 2-3 hours instead of 15+ hours.

The sales may be modest, but calculate your hourly rate. That $27 product took only 2 hours to create—earning me $13.50/hour. Compare that to a $50 product that required 15 hours and earned just $3.33/hour. Clear win.

Day 25-26: The Direct Feedback Request. Ask your customers directly what they want. Post in a Facebook group inquiring about their challenges. Send an email asking what they wish you offered. Reach out to past customers to learn about their experiences.

You may receive feedback that stings or requests you can't fulfill. However, you will also gain insights that will inform your next profitable product.

Day 27-28: The Visibility Push. Do something that increases your visibility in your industry. Start that YouTube channel you've been considering. Apply for a podcast interview. Share your expertise in a new forum or group.

They may not respond immediately, and you might feel awkward at first. But visibility is a muscle that strengthens with practice.

Day 29-30: The Integration Plan. Spend the final two days reviewing everything you learned and crafting a plan for sustaining this approach beyond the 30 days.

Which simple products outperformed complex ones? What uncomfortable practices are you ready to continue? How will you maintain momentum without overthinking?

Week 4 Integration Questions:

- Which simple experiments yielded the best return on time invested?
- What customer feedback surprised you most?
- How has your view of perfectionism versus progress evolved?
- What will you launch next without overthinking?

By the end of 30 days, failure wasn't something I avoided—it became a tool I utilized. The more I tried, the more I learned. And the more I learned, the more confident I became.

My 30-Day Transformation

When I began this challenge, I was paralyzed by perfectionism and afraid to share anything that might not work flawlessly. I spent more time planning than doing and more time researching than creating.

By Day 30, I had:

- Launched three simple products without overthinking.
- Raised my prices and gained confidence in my value.
- Started conversations with potential collaborators.
- Built an email list by actively inviting people to join.
- Created content that felt authentic rather than polished.

The numbers weren't the real victory—though they were encouraging. The true victory was the shift from asking, "What if this doesn't work?" to "What can I learn from this?"

The most unexpected outcome: I actually began enjoying the process of experimenting instead of dreading the possibility of failure.

Your 30-Day Challenge Action Plan

Before You Start:

- Set up a simple tracking system (even just a notebook).
- Inform someone about your challenge for accountability.

- Remind yourself that the goal is learning, not succeeding.

During the Challenge:

- Document your attempts and what you learn.
- Celebrate attempts, not just outcomes.
- Adjust the exercises to suit your business and comfort level.
- Remember that small failures are better than inaction.

After the Challenge:

- Review your biggest lessons and breakthrough moments.
- Identify which experiments you want to continue or scale.
- Plan your next 30 days of intentional growth.
- Share your experience to inspire others to start their own challenge.

The most important rule: There are no wrong answers, only learning opportunities.

If You are a Beginner and Need a Little More Support with Getting Started

Don't have a business yet? No problem! I have created a special Beginner's 30-Day Challenge Calendar designed specifically for those still figuring out their direction.

This simplified version focuses on discovery, skill identification, and building confidence through small daily actions. You will explore the problems you naturally solve, test market interest, and lay the foundation for your future business—all without the pressure of having everything figured out.

Download the Beginner's 30-Day Challenge Calendar to embark on your entrepreneurial journey with activities tailored for complete beginners.

<u>Download Your FREE 30-Day Challenge Calendar</u>

Scan the QR code or visit the link above to get instant access to your templates.

Once you complete the beginner challenge and identify your business direction, you can return to the full 30-Day Challenge above to accelerate your growth.

Remember: every successful entrepreneur started exactly where you are right now. The only difference is they took the first step.

The Challenge That Changes Everything

What would you attempt today if you weren't afraid to fail? Start there. That's Day 1.

This 30-day challenge isn't really about failure at all. It's about courage. It's about expanding your tolerance for uncertainty and your appetite for growth. It's about discovering that the things you are afraid to try are often the things you most need to do.

Every successful entrepreneur has undertaken a version of this challenge, whether they called it that or not. They've practiced taking action despite uncertainty. They've embraced course corrections. They've learned to view setbacks as setups. The difference is, they figured it out through years of painful trial and error. This challenge condenses that learning into 30 focused days.

Your business is waiting for you on the other side of your comfort zone. The ideas you are hesitant to test, the prices you are afraid to charge, the people you are reluctant to contact, the content you are scared to share—these aren't obstacles to your success. They are the stepping stones to it.

Your future self is waiting. All you have to do is begin.

CHAPTER 11
Stacking Failures, Building Foundations

Turning Losses into Leverage

After months of disappointing sales numbers and comparing myself to other entrepreneurs' highlight reels, I was celebrating all the wrong things. If I wanted to survive this journey, I needed to stop fearing failure and start designing a failure-friendly future.

Everyone was posting about their six-figure launches, their viral content, their perfect client testimonials. And there I was, feeling like a failure because my high-quality products weren't selling despite all my hard work.

I had been in this frustrating period for months. No matter how hard I worked, I couldn't seem to fix the problem. I just kept failing and failing. The constant disappointment affected my relationships at home—I was taking my anger and frustration out on the people I loved most.

Finally, I talked to my husband about it. I wanted sympathy, validation, someone to acknowledge how unfair it all was. Instead, with a huge smile on his face, he said, "Good. That means you are learning something."

I was furious with him. I left the conversation angry and hurt. How dare he say "good" when I was clearly struggling? But how can you get mad at someone who offers feedback with a smile and a calm demeanor? Well, I sure did.

Later, his words prompted reflection. I wanted someone to feel sorry for me, but what he said was actually what I needed to hear. No one was going to save me in business. There was no superman or superwoman who could swoop in and fix the situation but me.

His response compelled me to stop seeking sympathy and start pursuing solutions. Instead of dwelling on why my products weren't selling, I shifted my focus to what each non-sale was teaching me about my market, messaging, and audience. Your failure-friendly future begins when you stop trying to avoid falls and start getting good at them.

Creating Support Systems: Finding Your Failure-Friendly Tribe

The hardest part about changing your relationship with failure isn't the mindset shift; it's doing it alone. When everyone around you views failure as something to hide, embracing it as something to celebrate becomes incredibly difficult. I learned this the hard way during my first year of entrepreneurship.

The isolation of being the only one "failing forward": The most challenging aspect wasn't the actual failing. It was being surrounded by people focused on obstacles rather than the opportunities presented. There are two types of people: those who see a problem and get stuck on why it can't be solved, and those who see a problem and take steps to find solutions. I don't have all the answers, but I have the willingness to figure them out.

I knew it wouldn't be perfect; in fact, I expected it to be messy. As the saying goes, we have to sink to swim. Or, as I like to say: we must fail to flourish.

But try explaining that to those who believe any setback is evidence to quit. When I shared what I learned from experiments that didn't work, I often got that look, the one that said, "See? This is why you should play it safe."

Please don't misunderstand me—I started there, and I still find myself in that mindset in some areas of my life. We just have to take baby steps to grow beyond it.

Sometimes it's best to work in isolation until you have the courage to ignore the comments and let them roll off you, or until your business speaks louder than their doubts. Then, people begin to respect what you are building.

Even in online business groups, I felt like an outsider. Everyone was posting their wins, breakthroughs, and success stories. Nobody was discussing the messy middle, the experiments that taught valuable lessons, or how failures were actually propelling them forward faster than playing it safe ever could.

During this silent phase, your strength, courage, and resilience are being forged. You are learning how to overcome. Once you conquer this challenge, other obstacles become more manageable. I relied on my faith to overcome this area, which I know I can draw upon in new phases of business.

Consider the self-made millionaires who say that if they had to start over, they know they would achieve millionaire status again. Why? Because they learned and applied lessons from their failures. Those past mistakes that kept us up at night built an unshakeable foundation. Now, we feel that any mountain that comes our way can be cast into the sea. With this type of faith, we can move mountains.

Here's how to build your support system:

- **Model failure-friendly language:** Instead of saying "My product launch failed," say "My product launch taught me that my audience prefers X over Y." By modeling failure-friendly language, you give others permission to do the same.

- **Find honest entrepreneurs:** Seek out people who share their real journeys, not just their highlight reels. Look for entrepreneurs who discuss their struggles, learning curves, and pivots. These are your people.

- **Create safe spaces for honest conversation:** Start a mastermind group, join accountability partnerships, or simply be the person who asks, "What are you learning from this?" rather than "What are you winning at?"

- **Celebrate learning milestones, not just financial ones:** When someone in your circle uncovers something significant about their audience or market, celebrate that insight just as much as you would a big sale.

- **Share your own failures strategically:** Share not for sympathy, but for connection. When you recount a flopped product that taught you something valuable, you help others reframe their own setbacks.

My vision for this failure-friendly community: Entrepreneurs who admit they'd rather make progress than appear perfect. People who celebrate experiments regardless of their success. Mentors who ask better questions about what you are learning instead of what you are earning.

This is what I'm building—a group of entrepreneurs who wear their business bruises like badges of honor, knowing each one represents courage in action.

Teaching Others: How Sharing Your Failures Multiplies Your Success

The most unexpected benefit of embracing my failures was discovering how much others needed to hear about them.

When you start sharing what you learned from setbacks instead of hiding them, something powerful happens. People realize they are not alone in their struggles. They see that successful individuals don't avoid failure; they learn from it faster.

The typical response when you share authentic failure stories: *"Thank you for being honest about this. I thought I was the only one struggling." "This makes me feel so much better about my own challenges." "Can you share more about how you figured out what to do differently?"*

Here's what I discovered: teaching others about your failures doesn't just help them; it multiplies your own success. The more I shared what I'd learned, the more I recognized that these small, vulnerable lessons were compounding into the foundation of my success.

Here's why sharing your failures creates a compound effect:

It forces you to extract the lesson. When you prepare to teach someone else what you learned from a setback, you must clarify what that lesson was. This deepens your own understanding.

It builds authentic authority. People trust leaders who've faced challenges more than those who seem to have always figured everything out. Your struggles make you relatable; your lessons make you valuable.

It creates connection. When you share a failure story, people not only learn from your experience—they feel less alone in their struggles. That connection lays the groundwork for lasting business relationships.

It generates new insights. When you recount your failure story, others often see lessons or applications you missed. Teaching becomes a collaborative learning experience.

It positions you as a guide, not a guru. Instead of being the person who never fails, you become the person who fails forward faster. That's much more helpful to those still learning.

The teaching framework that works:

Share the context: What were you trying to achieve?

Describe what happened: What was the actual outcome?

Extract the lesson: What did you learn that you didn't know before?

Apply the insight: How are you using this lesson going forward?

Invite engagement: What similar experiences have others had?

The most powerful thing about learning how to fail forward is this: you don't keep it to yourself. When you model resilience, you give others permission to do the same. And then they pass it on. That's the multiplier effect—your growth becomes a ripple that touches people you'll never even meet.

Your one lesson creates a ripple that helps countless entrepreneurs reframe their own setbacks. And here's the business benefit nobody talks about: people buy from teachers they trust. When you share your real journey, including the messy parts, you build the kind of trust that turns followers into customers and customers into advocates.

But here's where sharing your failures gets really powerful. It creates a compound effect that builds over time.

The Compound Effect: How Today's Failures Become Tomorrow's Advantages

If I could go back and talk to my earlier self during those discouraging first months, I would tell her this: "Everything you think is going wrong right now is actually going right. You just can't see it yet." Here's how the compound effect of failure actually works: Every setback is a masterclass you didn't know you signed up for. Those lessons accumulate. Stack. Build on each other.

Eventually, the wisdom gained from all your "failures" becomes your secret weapon.

What the compound effect looks like in real life:

Customer insight accumulation: Each product that flops teaches you something gold about your audience's true desires. Within six months, you develop an almost supernatural sense of what will resonate.

Process refinement: Each clunky launch shows you exactly how to streamline systems. Problems that once took weeks to solve become manageable in hours.

Resilience building: Each setback that doesn't break you strengthens your backbone for the next challenge. Obstacles that would have paralyzed you in month one become minor speed bumps by year two.

Network expansion: Each "failure" story you share connects you with other entrepreneurs in the trenches. Your network grows through vulnerability, not just victory.

Skill diversification: Every unexpected outcome forces you to acquire new superpowers. You develop a Swiss Army knife of abilities that serves you everywhere.

Here's the timeline most people miss: The benefits of your failures often take six months to two years to fully manifest. That service that seemed "too complex"? It teaches you about simplicity, which later influences how you create products that sell consistently.

That promotion strategy that didn't take off?

It pushed you to think critically, tighten your message, and build systems that create lasting results. Because here's what's true:

Success is shaped by setbacks. Each misstep holds a lesson your competitors may never discover. Each adjustment makes you more responsive, more resilient, and more ready for what's next. What feels like slow progress is often the groundwork for breakthroughs.

Setbacks are part of the path—not signs you've lost your way. The question isn't *if* you will face them. It's how you will use them.

Every entrepreneur who's built something meaningful has a portfolio of lessons earned through real experience. The difference between those who give up and those who grow is that they extract the lesson, refine the vision, and keep moving.

You now hold everything you need to create a future rooted in wisdom, courage, and clarity.

You have learned to read the season you're in and adjust with intention. You have discovered how to protect what matters while still pushing forward. You understand that confusion, discomfort, and course corrections are often signs that you are expanding into new territory. Your failures are evidence that you're in the arena, doing the work, building something that matters.

Now, the only question is:

Where will you go from here?

Your Invitation to Fail Forward

Choose What Serves You, Not What Overwhelms You

You have been given plenty of tools: practical strategies, mindset shifts, and real-world examples. You don't need to apply them all at once. Pick the one that speaks to your season. Apply one shift. Take one step. Let that small win compound. Growth happens when clarity meets action. Not when we chase perfection, but when we move forward consistently.

I'm writing these final words on a Tuesday morning, one week after finishing my last day as a teacher to pursue a dream that felt too big and too scary to even articulate. There are bills on my desk, my Etsy sales from yesterday were modest, and I'm still figuring out what this new life looks like. It doesn't feel like failure because I have redefined success. To me, success now means forward motion, not flawless outcomes. By the old standards I learned in school, this should feel like failure. Instead, it feels like flying.

But here's the truth: the end of this book isn't the end of your journey. It's the beginning of your decision. You've seen what's possible. You've read real stories. You've learned strategies that work. Now, it's your turn to choose what comes next.

There are only two paths from here—and one of them leads to the version of yourself you've been hoping to become.

This is where theory becomes transformation. You have a choice: keep waiting for the perfect moment, or move forward in progress, even if it's messy. These are your two paths:

The Choice: Perfect Paralysis vs. Imperfect Progress

You've reached a decision point. You can either keep chasing perfection and stay stuck or take one imperfect step forward and build momentum. What you choose right now determines how your next chapter begins. This moment is your turning point.

Path One: Perfect Paralysis

You wait until you have all the answers, skills, confidence, and guarantees. You research, plan, and prepare until you feel completely ready. You avoid anything that might not work perfectly the first time.

This path feels safe, but it's actually the riskiest choice you can make. While you are waiting to be ready, opportunities are passing you by. By avoiding small failures, you are guaranteeing one massive failure: the failure to ever discover what you are truly capable of.

Path Two: Imperfect Progress

You start before you feel ready. You experiment with incomplete information. You risk small failures in service of big dreams. You get comfortable being uncomfortable.

This path feels scary, but it's actually the safest choice you can make. Every small failure teaches you something valuable. Every experiment moves you closer to what works. Every mistake makes you smarter for the next attempt. You don't need a perfect plan. You need a decision. And you just made one.

I spent three years on Path One. I had notebooks full of business ideas, browser bookmarks full of research, and a head full of reasons why I wasn't ready yet. I was preparing to succeed instead of actually succeeding.

Everything changed when I chose Path Two. Not because I stopped being afraid, but because I stopped letting fear dictate my decisions.

The entrepreneurs you admire, the businesses you look up to, the success stories that inspire you? They all chose Path Two. They all started before they felt ready.

Your Permission Slip: Official Authorization to Make Mistakes

For too many years, I waited for someone to give me permission to fail.

That permission never came. The people who could have given it were playing by the same broken rules I was. They were trapped in the same system that values looking good over learning.

So I'm giving you the permission slip I wish someone had given me:

You have permission to start before you feel ready and experiment with uncertain outcomes.

You have permission to fail spectacularly and learn magnificently.

You have permission to change direction when you discover new information.

You have permission to value progress over perfection and choose learning over looking good.

You have permission to disappoint those who expect you to play it safe.

You have permission to succeed in ways that don't resemble anyone else's success.

Most importantly, you have permission to fail forward faster than anyone expects, including yourself.

This isn't just motivational rhetoric. This is official authorization from someone who has walked this path, who has paid the price of both playing it safe and taking risks, and who has discovered that the cost of not failing is higher than the cost of failing forward.

Sign your name here: _____

Date: _____

Now you are officially authorized to make the mistakes that will lead you to success.

This Wasn't Written from the Finish Line

Most business books are written by people who are already ten chapters ahead—far removed from the messy middle you're still navigating. And while their wisdom is valuable, it can sometimes feel unreachable.

This book? It was written in real time. Not after I "made it," but while I was still building, still failing, still figuring things out. These aren't polished strategies from the mountaintop. They're field notes from the climb—tested during quiet launches, disappointing sales, unexpected wins, and slow but steady growth.

Wherever you are starting, scaling, or stumbling, I wrote this to remind you: *you're not behind.* Your path is valid. And you already have what it takes to keep going.

The Ripple Effect: How Your Failure Journey Inspires Others

Here's something beautiful that happens when you start failing forward: you give other people permission to do the same.

When you share what you learned from a setback, someone else realizes they're not alone.

When you celebrate an imperfect attempt, someone else finds the courage to try.

When you treat failures as valuable data, someone else starts seeing their setbacks differently. Your willingness to fail forward creates waves of possibility that reach people you may never meet.

You are not just building a business; you are building a movement.

My Promise:
What Happens When You Embrace This Mindset

I can't promise you instant success. I can't promise you that everything will work perfectly. I can't promise you that failing forward will be easy or comfortable or applauded by everyone around you.

But I can promise you this:

Embrace failure as your teacher instead of your enemy, and you will learn faster than you ever thought possible. Every setback becomes a shortcut to wisdom. Every mistake becomes a competitive advantage.

Start taking action despite uncertainty, and you will discover capabilities you didn't know you had. You'll solve problems you thought were too big for you. You'll create solutions you never imagined. You'll become the person who can handle whatever your business throws at you.

Choose progress over perfection, and you will outpace competitors who are still waiting to be ready. While they're perfecting their business plans, you'll be perfecting your business through real-world experience.

Share your real journey, and you will build deeper connections than you thought possible. Customers will trust you because you are honest about the learning process. Peers will respect you because you are secure enough to admit what you don't know.

You are not supposed to have it all figured out yet.

Your value isn't in perfection—it's in your perspective. There is no one in the world exactly like you. The talent you carry, the story you hold, and the way you solve problems are unique to you. And the only way to refine that gift is through practice. That's the journey of becoming—not just doing business, but becoming the kind of person who can lead, create, and sustain it.

This transformation is real. I've lived it.

The person who was once too scared to launch a simple course is now writing a book about failing forward. The teacher who was paralyzed by perfectionism is now helping others embrace their mistakes.

This isn't magic. This is mindset.

And mindset can be changed through the beautiful act of imperfect action.

Your Multiple Pathways Forward

You now have everything you need to start failing forward today.

If you are overwhelmed by possibilities: Start with the 30-Day Failure Challenge. Pick Day 1. Do it today.

If perfectionism is your enemy: Launch something simple this week. The goal isn't success—it's practice.

If you feel isolated: Find one person who will celebrate your attempts, not just your achievements.

If you are avoiding an experiment: Test it with the smallest possible investment. Ten dollars. Two hours. One post.

If you are ready to lead: Share one failure story and what you learned. Your vulnerability gives others permission too.

You don't need to choose every strategy. Choose what resonates with where you are right now.

Growth happens at every level. Every small step counts.

Your Failing Forward Future

Close your eyes and imagine this:

It's one year from today. You are reviewing your business progress.

You've launched six products. Three were huge successes. Two taught you valuable lessons about your market. One revealed a completely new direction you never would have discovered without the willingness to experiment.

You make decisions quickly because you've learned to view uncertainty as data collection rather than a cause for paralysis.

While your competitors are still in the planning phase, you are already in the profit phase.

You've built genuine relationships with customers who trust you because you've been honest about your learning journey.

You've helped other entrepreneurs fail forward by sharing your real story.

Most importantly, you've become the person who can handle whatever comes next. Not because you have all the answers, but because you know how to find them.

This isn't fantasy. This is what happens when you embrace failure as your competitive advantage.

Five years from now, you'll look back on today's failures as pivotal moments. The flop that revealed your true market. The misstep that identified your ideal customer. The failure that led you to the strategy that finally worked.

Your failure portfolio will be your most valuable business asset.

Your Next Right Step

The book is ending, but your story is just beginning.

You have the principles. Failure is data, not defeat. Progress trumps perfection. Learning matters more than looking good.

You have the frameworks. The challenges, feedback loops, and mindset shifts that transform setbacks into stepping stones.

You have permission. Official authorization to make mistakes, experiment, learn, grow, and become the entrepreneur you are meant to be.

The only thing left is action.

So here's my final invitation:

What will you try today that might not work perfectly but will definitely teach you something valuable?

What experiment will you start this week that might fail spectacularly but could also succeed beyond your wildest dreams?

What risk will you take this month that scares you just enough to make you grow?

Your failing forward future is waiting. It's waiting for you to stop planning and start doing. To stop preparing and start participating. To stop avoiding failure and start embracing it as your greatest teacher.

The entrepreneurs who change the world aren't the ones who never fall down.

They're the ones who get really good at getting back up.

Your moment is now. Your permission is granted. Your future is calling.

What are you waiting for?

Go fail forward. I'll be cheering you on from here.

With faith in your failing forward future,
Katyya Moses

P.S. This isn't about loving failure—it's about daring to fail in service of something bigger than fear. It's about choosing growth over comfort, one imperfect step at a time.

Your story isn't written yet. But it starts with your next brave move.

Make it count.

Resources to Support Your Journey

You don't have to walk this road alone. Whether you're just starting out or navigating the messy middle, these tools were created to help you take meaningful steps forward—no matter what stage you're in.

The Failure Portfolio (PDF Workbook)

A companion workbook designed to help you turn setbacks into strategies. Use it to document what's not working, reflect on what you've learned, and build your next move with clarity.

Download it here:

https://katyyamoses.myflodesk.com/failureportfolio

The 30-Day Challenge (PDF)

This no-fluff challenge gives you one small action a day to build momentum in your business. It's designed for clarity, consistency, and confidence.

Download it here:

https://katyyamoses.myflodesk.com/30daychallenge

Done-for-You Digital Products (Resellable)

If you're unsure what to sell, this collection of editable digital products with Master Resell Rights helps you start quickly, without having to create from scratch.

Browse the collection: www.elevatehervault.com and www.katyyamoses.com

How to Hire Your Kid (Course)

Want to keep your business in the family and teach your kids valuable skills? This course shows you how to legally hire your child, save on taxes, and build generational wealth.

Access the course: www.hireyourkidstoday.com

Watch & Grow with Me on YouTube

I share real-time business lessons, behind-the-scenes strategies, and encouragement for entrepreneurs building imperfectly.

www.youtube.com/@katyyamoses

Not Sure Where to Start?

Start small. Choose one tool that meets your current needs. Come back to the rest as you grow.

Progress is built through action—and you've already begun.

About the Author

Katyya Moses is a wife, mom of three, and former special-education teacher who turned her biggest failures into the foundation for a thriving entrepreneurial life. After years of playing it safe inside classrooms in Mississippi, Texas, and Kuwait, she walked away from the traditional career path and built multiple successful digital-product businesses from the ground up.

Through books like The Failure Portfolio, she equips readers with practical frameworks, faith-filled mindset shifts, and real-world strategies to turn setbacks into momentum. When she isn't writing or mentoring entrepreneurs, Katyya is cheering on her children, exploring new creative projects, and showing families that courageous living—and lasting success—begin on the other side of fear.

www.ingramcontent.com/pod-product-compliance
Lightning Source LLC
Chambersburg PA
CBHW071552210326
41597CB00019B/3212